D0707601

Real
Nordic
Living

Dorothea Gundtoft

Real Nordic Living

Design. Food. Art. Travel.

with over 300 illustrations

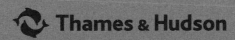
Thames & Hudson

Contents

A Nordic Life

INTRODUCTION

There is something endurably alluring about Nordic living – to non-Scandinavians, at least. From the mid-century furniture designs of Finn Juhl and Arne Jacobsen to the latest creations from the New Nordic cuisine scene, the democratic social structures to the breathtaking natural beauty of its landscapes, life in the far north can seem an enviable prospect, indeed.

The reality, of course, is a little different. With the sun disappearing for weeks on end, and the cold and damp of the long winters seeping into one's bones, it is perhaps natural for a certain melancholy to creep into the national character – possibly explaining why the Scandinavians are so good at their particularly dark take on crime thrillers, both in book

form and on television. And yet, even with the weather and a morbid taste in fiction, the Scandinavians seem to have cracked it, with lifestyles (and soft furnishings) that are the envy of the world. Not for nothing is Ikea the first stop for many when furnishing a student flat or a new home.

Together, the Nordic countries – Denmark, Sweden and Norway – consistently rank among the highest internationally in terms of happiness, with Denmark leading the way (although recently supplanted by Norway) and Copenhagen regularly named happiest city. They offer generous holiday allowances and parental leave, health care and education for all – paid for, admittedly, by some of the highest taxes in the world.

This hefty price tag, however, ensures that the focus is fixed firmly on equality, with Sweden recognized as the most gender-equal country of them all. There is also a democratic approach in all of the Nordic countries to a modest form of luxury, made available to their residents via a good standard of living across the board. You don't see many Ferraris, but you do see plenty of Volvos, more suited to the important Scandinavian principles of family life and togetherness.

But apart from the happiness and the equality – both wonderful things – the real secret of Nordic living and its enduring appeal (and most cited by the designers, makers and creatives in this book) is that oft-used word, *hygge*. Although its description as the ultimate lifestyle is bemusing to many Scandinavians, they readily admit that during those long winters, it's what keeps them going. Something delicious to eat and drink, a comfortable chair, a cosy fire: these are the essentials of *hygge*. But most important of all is sharing these moments with the people you love. (*Uhygge* represents the other extreme, with those crime thrillers being a prime example.)

Because Scandinavians spend so much time indoors, their homes have become the centre of their world – perhaps why their interiors are so appealing. They are enticing because they have to be. *Real Nordic Living* meets those designers and makers who create *hygge* in their homes every day, with food, in the outdoors, in art, architecture and fashion. Nordic living isn't about – or not entirely about – soft furnishings or enviable furniture design. It isn't even, really, about *hygge*. It's about taking care of what's around you, and that includes your home.

Being kind to yourself, your surroundings and those around you is a surer path to happiness than any scatter cushion or paint colour can provide. But we recognize that these things make us happy, too. Life is too complicated to deny the restorative feel-good power of a beautifully designed chair.

So take inspiration from the creatives featured here: try out a new recipe or a new craft, head out into the countryside or your local park for a walk or a picnic, pick a bunch of flowers for the table, have friends round for lunch, or just enjoy the simple pleasure of rearranging your books or collection of vases in a pleasing way. Taking the time to enjoy things, to *care* about them, including yourself, is the key to really living the Nordic life.

Above all, have a *hyggelig* time!

Design
&
Interiors

Anne-Louise Sommer

As curator and director of the
Danish Museum of Art and Design in
Copenhagen, Anne-Louise Sommer is
a firm believer in the importance of good
design to our surroundings, and in the
democratic availability of it to everyone.
She is the author of several books on
design, including a monograph on the
watercolours of Finn Juhl.

From the very start of her career, Anne-Louise Sommer has worked in the fields of design and architecture, as a teacher and researcher, and as head of research at the Royal Danish Academy of Fine Arts in Copenhagen. In 2011 she became the director of the Danish Museum of Art and Design, a position she continues to hold today.

'I'm very driven by social awareness and the desire to better the lives of as many people as possible,' she says. 'The potential of design to improve one's life is a very appealing idea. As a child, my parents' love of design had a significant impact on me. Growing up in a well-designed environment certainly makes a difference, and has reinforced my belief in the importance of making sure everyone has access to it. Denmark has benefited from good design, at every scale, for many years. Here, good design is for everyone, reflecting our traditions of democracy and welfare.'

Anne-Louise, what designs do you consider among Scandinavia's greatest achievements?

It is hard to point to a single design object. I have my favourites, of course, but I really believe that the most significant contribution Scandinavian design has made to the world is our attitude towards it, an awareness that also has a political and historical context. In the 1920s and '30s things were very difficult in Denmark, but this is the period when the best schools and public spaces were being built. Just think of Poul Henningsen's lighting systems, the state-of-the-art furniture designs of Hans J. Wegner and Børge Mogensen, and housing in general: well-equipped two-room apartments, surrounded by greenery and playgrounds. The government didn't have any money, but they made a conscious decision to invest for the long term in good design. My own office is filled with furniture made by Kaare Klint 85 years ago, for Thorvald Stauning, Denmark's first socialist prime minster.

'In Denmark good design is for all, reflecting our traditions of democracy and looking after each other.'

How is working with established designers different from working with students?

It makes perfect sense to combine new talent with established designers. Here, we aim to connect the classics with contemporary design and themes that address issues that are relevant to our lives today. There is a lot of young talent on the Danish design scene, and we have a close connection to the Royal Danish Academy of Fine Arts. We have held several events in collaboration with various schools, and aim to be a place where visitors from both Denmark and further afield can experience the latest trends in Danish design and crafts. Our focus will always remain on our great historical collections, which demonstrate the history of different styles, ideas and techniques within the field of Danish design.

Do you believe that the concept of hygge *has led to the development of design in this country?*

We get a lot of questions about this in the museum! Danes have a knack for furnishing their homes in a way that can appear cosy, stylish and relaxed. My experience is that Danish design is deeply rooted in our way of living. We know our classics and have an appreciation for quality materials and craftsmanship. Light is very important to those of us who live in northern Europe, where the winters are long and dark. You can see this in hotels and restaurants, as well as in private homes. The home of one of our most important designers, Finn Juhl (p. 34), now a part of Ordrupgaard museum (p. 198), is a wonderful example of the interrelation between furniture design and modern art. The colour palette in his house is extraordinary, and very modern for its time.

Artilleriet Interiors

This elegant and inspirational shop in Gothenburg proves that Stockholm isn't Sweden's only leading design destination. A must for anyone wishing to recreate the look and feel of a cosy Nordic interior in their own home.

Artilleriet, founded by Christian Duivenvoorden and Sofie Hellsing in 2011, offers everyone from interior design professionals to enthusiastic amateurs an eclectic collection of furniture and accessories, with vintage and contemporary pieces displayed alongside innovative design from around the world. The company works with well-known brands, including homegrown labels Muuto and Hay, along with international designers such as Tom Dixon and Comme des Garçons. A second shop, The Kitchen, is located next door.

Sofie, Gothenburg is perhaps not the most obvious choice of location for a design shop. What was the vision behind Artilleriet?

We had a shop in our minds, a place where inspiration played a central role. It would be a space where we could create unexpected combinations of products without following the usual rules of interior design, and where we could showcase some of the amazing creative brands we found from all over the world. As far as the location is concerned, we love Gothenburg. We were born here, and definitely followed our hearts instead of our heads. It's the same way we choose our products: we are driven by a passion for beautiful, smart design with a story to tell. And Sweden is more than just Stockholm!

How do you recreate that famous Nordic cosiness in your own home and in your shop?

For Scandinavians, our home is the most important place: it is where we are social, hang with our families and are free to be ourselves. Because it is dark and cold outside for most of the year, we want to have a cosy, warm home. Designers are important,

but sometimes the interior designers and stylists, the ones that make good design come to life, get forgotten. Ilse Crawford (see Ett Hem; p. 226), in particular, has a way of thinking about interiors that we can relate to, and Dimorestudio in Milan is another favourite. In Sweden, we've grown up with the idea of *hygge*. We achieve it by creating a welcoming atmosphere at home, which is reflected in our store and in the designs we sell. It's how we Scandinavians get the best out of the places we live in.

Bjørn Wiinblad

Artist and designer Bjørn Wiinblad (1918–2006) is a
revered name in Danish ceramics, and his 'Romance'
dinner set for the Rosenthal porcelain company is an
essential part of any Nordic placesetting. Today, his
distinctive, colourful designs are highly collectible, and
can be found in the permanent collections of museums
around the world, including the V&A in London and
MoMA in New York.

Having studied at the Royal Danish Academy of Fine Arts in Copenhagen and worked in the studio of ceramicist Lars Syberg, Wiinblad branched out on his own in 1952. His first one-man show was held just two years later in the USA. In 1965, he collaborated on the costumes and set designs for a production of *The Tempest* at the Dallas Theater Center, and acted as a co-director.

But it was his work for the Rosenthal porcelain company, particularly the 'Romance' dinner set and a series of commemorative Christmas plates beginning in 1971, which ensured that Wiinblad's highly distinctive, self-taught style of strong colours and romantic imagery would become recognized around the world.

Wiinblad was also a famed poster designer and illustrator, and produced designs for the Olympic Games and the Royal Danish Ballet, as well as illustrations for an edition of the stories of Hans Christian Andersen.

Finn Juhl

Finn Juhl's House

Designer and architect Finn Juhl (1912–1989) was one of
the key members of the Danish Modern movement, along
with Arne Jacobsen, Hans J. Wegner, Poul Kjærholm and
Kaare Klint. In 1942, he designed a house and studio for
himself and his family in Ordrup, outside Copenhagen.
The house, open to the public since 2008, has since become
recognized as the embodiment of Nordic design.

'Furniture and houses are, of course, always designed in a context,' Juhl said in 1982. 'I have rarely built a house where I didn't also design the furniture. It is fundamental that the furniture is practical – chairs are not designed to look at but to sit on, after all – but it makes us happy if they are also worth looking at.'

For his own house, originally shared with his first wife Inge-Marie Skaarup, Juhl followed the same principles, creating a relationship between the building and the furniture and works of art inside it. He designed all of the furniture, with much of it handcrafted by Niels Vodder for the Cabinetmakers' Guild Exhibition in 1937.

In 1930, at the age of 18, Juhl had visited the Stockholm Exhibition and seen the work of architect Erik Gunnar Asplund. Although he admired Asplund's mathematical approach, Juhl was not interested in designing furniture that was purely functional. Instead, he produced vividly sculptural forms that reflected his interest in abstract art. Among the most widely recognized of his furniture designs today are the 'FJ45' and 'Høvdingestolen' chairs; simpler, industrially produced chair designs include 'Japan' and 'Karmstolen'. Juhl intended his furniture to be seen from all angles, and would often place it in the centre of the room, away from the walls.

The house itself is made from brick and covered in a grey-white render, which gives it a soft, matte effect and creates a strong contrast between the gleaming white building and the dark woodland beyond. Inside, the layout is an early example of a Scandinavian open-plan dwelling, with each zone having a distinct function. The ceilings

are painted in a pale yellow, reflecting the light from outside. In the corner of the living room is a portrait of Juhl's second wife, Hanne Wilhelm Hansen (above), by the Danish modernist painter Vilhelm Lundstrøm. Having initially wanted to study art history, Juhl remained an enthusiastic collector, and acquired works by Alvar Aalto, Sonja Ferlov Mancoba, Asger Jorn and Erik Thommesen, among others. Outside, the garden was designed by landscape architect Troels Erstad. Now part of the Ordrupgaard museum (p. 198), the house has an important place in Danish design history, and gives visitors a glimpse into the design ideas that would later coalesce into the movement known as Scandinavian Modern.

'One cannot create happiness with beautiful objects, but one can spoil quite a lot of happiness with bad ones.'

Flora Danica

One of the most magnificent porcelain services ever created in Scandinavia is 'Flora Danica', first produced in 1790 by Royal Copenhagen and still in production today. Considered among the finest examples of porcelain design in the world, Flora Danica is a beloved national design symbol of Denmark.

In 1761, the Danish king Frederik V commissioned a botanical encyclopedia, an enormous undertaking that comprised dozens of volumes and thousands of hand-tinted engravings of Danish wildflowers, represented in astonishing detail. It was not completed until 1883. In 1790 a dinner set, based on the encyclopedia, was commissioned from Royal Copenhagen by Frederik's grandson, Crown Prince Frederik, who had ordered it as a present for Catherine II of Russia (unfortunately, Catherine died in 1796 and never saw it).

The dinner set, like the encyclopedia, was to include every wild plant in Denmark at the time. Johann Christoph Bayer, an employee of Royal Copenhagen from 1776 to 1802, spent 12 years painting the decorations and miniature detail of the nearly two thousand pieces of porcelain, conducting his research

at the Botanical Garden in Copenhagen and sending an assistant out to draw any detail he might have missed or to ensure the correct colour of a single leaf. Most of the original service remains in the Danish Royal Family, and is on display at Rosenborg Castle in Copenhagen. Seventy years later, a second set was made for Princess Alexandra of Denmark on the occasion of her marriage to the Prince of Wales, later Edward VII, in 1863.

Today, Flora Danica is made to order by Royal Copenhagen, founded in 1775 by Frantz Heinrich Müller, and remains as popular as ever. The company's distinctive factory mark of three waved lines, representing the three straits of Denmark – Øresund, Lille Bælt and Store Bælt – is still used today, and is a reminder of the longstanding tradition of Nordic ceramics.

Josef Frank

Austrian-born architect and designer
Josef Frank (1885–1967) was also
a co-founder of the Vienna School
of Architecture. After emigrating
to Sweden in 1933, he joined
textile firm Svenskt Tenn, where
he produced some of the defining
designs of Swedish Modernism.
In 2017, an exhibition devoted to
Frank's work was held at the Fashion
and Textile Museum in London.

Having begun a new life in Sweden, Frank became the in-house designer at Svenskt Tenn the following year. The company had been set up by Estrid Ericson (1894–1981), an art teacher who wanted to offer pewter objects at reasonable prices. Using an inheritance from her father, she began producing her pewter designs at the back of the shop, and her creative vision paid off when Svenskt Tenn won the gold medal at the 1925 Paris Exhibition.

While at the company, Frank created some of its most recognizable and best-loved textile, wallpaper and furniture designs. He soon abandoned architecture altogether, and produced over two thousand furniture sketches and hundreds of textile designs for Svenskt Tenn. Over the next 30 years Frank and Ericson created a formidable working collaboration, with Frank producing designs for furniture and textiles, and Ericson providing the creative vision. Together they transformed Swedish design, which had previously been somewhat cold and formal, into something more colourful, eclectic and stylish. Josef Frank's designs remain popular today, and are an integral part of Sweden's design heritage.

'There's nothing wrong with mixing old and new, combining furniture styles, colours and patterns. Things that you like will fuse to form a relaxing entity.'

Josephine Akvama Hoffmeyer

Josephine Akvama Hoffmeyer, former creative director of Made a Mano, supplies handcrafted ceramic tiles, wallpapers and paints to Copenhagen's budding interior designers through her design company File Under Pop. Following her lead, a new generation of homeowners is turning its back on traditional white walls and pastel shades in favour of bold colours and graphic schemes.

Hot on the heels of its successful first two years of business, File Under Pop is about to expand internationally. 'We are able to handle both contract and retail, which gives us options in other countries,' explains Josephine. 'Currently, we are working with private residences, restaurants and hotels in different parts of the world. I am on my way to Uruguay, where we are decorating an entire villa with paint, tiles, lava stones and wallpaper, which is great fun.'

A native of Copenhagen, Josephine was raised by a Danish mother and a Ghanaian father, and the design traditions of both countries remain a potent source of inspiration. 'My early childhood unfolded in the 1970s, which meant lots of colours, patterns and style,' she says. 'The colours used in our home were primarily orange, purple and reddish brown. Leather couches, smoky mirrors, glass tables with gilded legs, Verner Panton-designed lamps and chairs were part of the interior. When I look back on it today, I associate it with bad taste, coupled with enthusiasm and playfulness. There were no rules whatsoever! Today, however, I find a lot of inspiration in my Ghanaian background.'

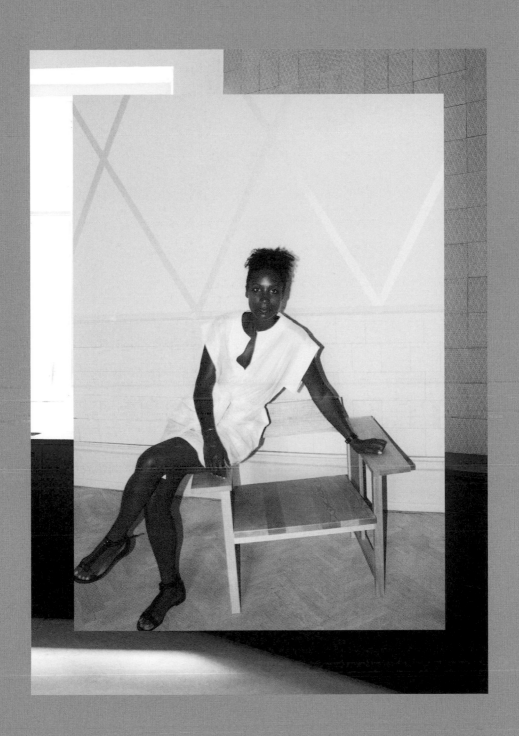

Josephine, how is your work day structured, and do you follow a set routine?

Each day, I ride my bike to the studio, and have a cup of coffee the minute I arrive. I sit down with colleagues to plan the day, then answer calls and emails from clients and suppliers. It's important for me to pick up my son from school and take him to football practice. Then I make dinner, and put him to bed. Normally I work until midnight, but in my fantasy life, I also meditate and do yoga.

What do you consider important when it comes to Nordic interior design?

Because of the long, cold winters, we tend to stay at home in the evenings. We don't go out as much as people in southern Europe, and use candles or soft lighting, plants and flowers to create that cosy atmosphere in our homes. I used to live in Italy, where they thought that candles only belonged in cemeteries! They associated cosiness with the opposite: going out, meeting friends.

In terms of colour, there is no such thing as an ugly or undesirable one: they all relate to one another. My focus is to find the connection between different colours and to balance their strengths and limitations. For the last 20 years, white has been the go-to colour in Nordic countries. If any other colour was used, it would be a pastel. But Danes are starting to want colour back in their lives again. I like to define a room with specific colours: fresh and cool hues in bedrooms; warmer, denser tones in the kitchen or living room. Doing this allows you to create *hygge* with paint in an easy, economical way. And you can even do it yourself, rather than hiring a decorator.

Do you have any favourite places that you make a beeline for when you need to relax?

I love to go hiking in Jotunheimen National Park in southern Norway. Closer to home, I often go to Jægersborg Dyrehave, a forest park north of the city, at the weekends to walk or cycle, watch the herds of deer go by or read a book. If I need more people around me, I'll head to the Christiania neighbourhood of Copenhagen or the Louisiana Museum of Modern Art (p. 190).

Mads Nørgaard

Third-generation fashion designer Mads Nørgaard heads up the iconic clothing brand established by his grandfather in 1944. He believes firmly that keeping production local is better for the environment, young people are our future, and a happy work environment is the key to success – values that are very much in tune with the Nordic way of life.

When Mads's father opened his own shop in the early 1960s, it was one of the first fashion stores in Denmark to recognize and engage with the emerging youth scene. As well as selling clothes, he also insisted on relating fashion to art, women's rights, and young people in general.

This socially conscious mindset has ensured an especially loyal staff, many of whom have been with the company for decades. 'One staff member has been with us for over 50 years, and two more for nearly 50 years, which is quite amazing,' he says. 'So there is a lot of history: the premises, employees, suppliers, furniture and traditions. I am very keen on history and continuity, but on the other hand, we almost never celebrate jubilees or the past. My focus is on the future. It's all about doing something that's relevant for tomorrow.'

Mads, with a Norwegian mum, did you grow up with some of the traditions of that country?

Being half-Norwegian, half-Danish is quite important to me. Although I do occasionally notice quite big differences between the Nordic countries, I see them much more as a homogenous whole when compared to the rest of the world, which somehow seems more separate. Scandinavia represents a cluster of youth culture, of togetherness. The essence of that togetherness is *hygge*, which is about having a good time, in a relaxing atmosphere. I do that naturally with friends and family. It's quite easy for me, perhaps it's different for people from other countries.

Now that you've incorporated art and social change into your brand, do you believe that this is the secret of your success?

My relationship to fashion is somewhat ambivalent. On the one hand, I am in love with everything new: new trends, designs, pop music, and so on. But on the other, I sometimes think that the 'new' comes at too fast a speed. Good things that are old are sometimes replaced before they are worn out – or even tried on. I feel this results in a superficial kind of consumerism that isn't appealing or healthy, for the consumers or for the environment. So between these two poles I try to find my path: in design, social structures and corporate social responsibility, with a touch of politics.

What does the future hold for the Nørgaard brand?

We have just opened two new shops on Tullinsgade in the Vesterbro area of Copenhagen, which only carry my own lines. It's great to see two spaces filled with my own stuff, which has been an ambition for a long time. We plan to open more shops, because it feels right. So, the plan is to always improve my designs, keeping the same price point and slowly improving fabrics, always inspired by the new and what kids are wearing today. Real clothing for real people, produced locally: that's what we strive for.

Marie Gudme Leth

One of the pioneers behind the revival of textile printing in Denmark in the 1930s, Marie Gudme Leth (1895–1997) produced designs that are reminiscent of those produced by Josef Frank (p. 44) and Svenskt Tenn. The warm colours of her designs are the essence of that timeless Scandinavian style.

Marie Gudme Leth was born in Aarhus, on the Jutland peninsula, where she honed her talent for drawing at the local technical school. She graduated from the School of Drawing and Art Industry in Copenhagen, later studying at the Royal Danish Academy of Fine Arts and working at the Danish Museum of Decorative Arts. When she began designing textiles in the 1920s, printed fabrics were rarely made in Denmark, as the artisanal craft of textile printing had not survived the influx of cheaper printed cottons from Europe.

In 1921, on a visit to Java in Indonesia, Leth was introduced to batik, the technique of wax-resist dyeing. Upon returning to Denmark three years later, she began showing her designs in group exhibitions in Copenhagen, and soon realized that there was a market for

beautiful, functional printed textiles. From the beginning, Leth's aim was to raise the status of printed textiles to that of other branches of the applied arts, and over the next 40 years she made a huge contribution to the resurgence in the production of high-quality, handcrafted goods.

Leth set up a workshop in 1941, and over the next few years designed some of her most celebrated patterns, including 'Kirsebær' (cherries), 'Frederiksberg Have' (Frederiksberg Gardens) and 'Indiens Blomster' (flowers of India). The lack of available materials during the war had an impact on textile printing. Although it was difficult to obtain pigments, dyes and basic fabrics, Leth succeeded in maintaining a reasonable level of production.

Throughout her nearly 40 years as a textile printer, Leth was able to adapt her style to changing tastes and technological innovations. The 1940s and '50s were productive years for the workshop, and her textiles became successful export items, particularly to the American and Canadian markets. Wherever her fabric designs were shown, they were enthusiastically received. Leth won a gold medal at the 1937 World's Fair in Paris, and another at the 1951 Triennale in Milan, and continued to produce printed textiles until closing her workshop in the 1960s.

Marie Gudme Leth's legacy has been as an educator (she taught pattern design and practical textile printing at the School of Applied Arts in Copenhagen until 1948) and mentor to the many student trainees who worked with her. Today she is recognized for the important role she played in encouraging and building a professional foundation for the generations of designers that followed her.

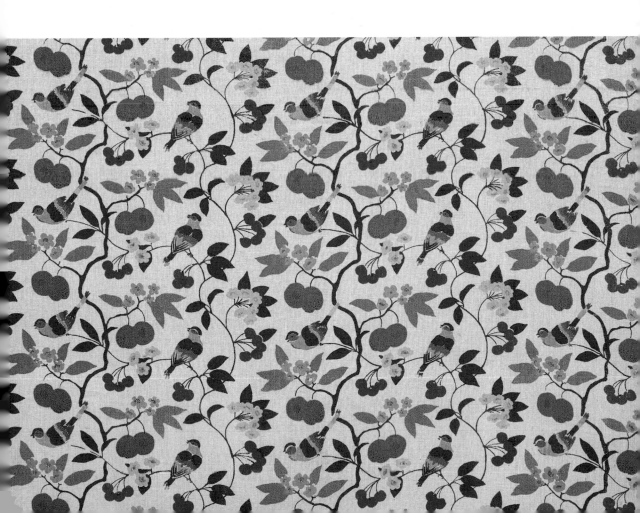

Skandinavisk

Englishman Shaun Russell has an outsider's view of what makes *hygge* so essential to wellbeing and happiness. Recognizing that one of the most potent images associated with *hygge* is flickering candlelight, he set up the lifestyle brand Skandinavisk, which provides ceramics and scented candles to those after a bit of Nordic living.

Shaun Russell's story is a modern tale for our globally connected times. While living in Sydney, Australia, he met his future wife, a Danish trainee doctor, who was studying at the University of Gothenburg. After a whirlwind courtship, Shaun arrived in Denmark for the first time 18 months later. The couple found an apartment in the Frederiksberg area of Copenhagen, where they stayed for next four years, got married and had their first child. A move to Stockholm followed, along with another child. Six years later, the family has returned to Copenhagen.

While all this was going on, Shaun worked for two different American corporations, and travelled extensively across Scandinavia – an experience, he says, which gave him a 'wonderful exposure' to the region as whole, as well as a better understanding of and appreciation for what makes Scandinavia so different to the rest of the world.

'Though I never will be Scandinavian, I think I might have a better idea about what Scandinavia is than many of its inhabitants,' Shaun explains. 'It is a tremendous benefit for people to grow up here, for all the advantages it offers.'

Shaun, where did the idea for launching Skandinavisk come from?

After living in Scandinavia for 10 years, I felt there was a very powerful story that hadn't been told yet – one of a balance of extremes, between the vast, empty landscapes and the emphasis on everyday happiness. It seemed to me that it is this balance that makes Scandinavia what it is, and why other countries look to it as a benchmark. In trying to work out how best to tell that story, the answer was sitting on the table in front of me: the candle. Adding fragrance just completed the story.

What are your impressions of hygge,
and of experiencing it in Denmark?

Hygge, for me, represents the Danish focus on achieving happiness through small, everyday moments, though I don't think any Dane would put it that way. *Hygge* isn't cool and it isn't discriminatory; it's universal, it will happen many times a day and you can't have too much of it. It is an unconscious embracing of life that the rest of the world could learn a lot from. In England we constantly defer happiness – to the weekend, holidays, a new car, a bigger house. We don't live in the moment, as we are too busy getting somewhere else, and I think most other developed nations are the same. But I don't think Danes have ownership of *hygge*; the Swedes and Norwegians are very good at prioritizing those moments, as well, they just have different words to express it: *mys*, *fika*, *kose*. It's just being continually held up as the world's happiest nation that makes Denmark the hero of the hour.

How do you develop new product ranges,
and what are some of your biggest markets?

We start by identifying an aspect of Scandinavia – whether a landscape or a feeling – which we believe is unique to the region, precious to its inhabitants, and perhaps intriguing to the outside world. We then develop a series of fragrance notes to bring it to life, and we always work to ensure that the final result speaks softly and with refinement – an aesthetic we appreciate in Scandinavian design – rather than shouts for attention. We then choose a local name and a carefully considered colour palette. The five Nordic countries (including Finland and Iceland) remain our largest regional market, but the UK is now our largest single market. We are also experiencing growth across Europe, into Asia, North America and Australia, so we are very excited that the world is waking up to the Scandinavian way of living. For us, connecting stories from Scandinavia with design and fragrance is something we love and intend to keep doing for many years to come.

Do you have further collaborations
in the pipeline?

We have done three collaborations so far, with Playtype, Illums Bolighus and Epal in Iceland. It is important when we work with other brands that there is a relevance to our partnership. Our colleagues at Playtype have been friends and neighbours since the beginning, and we offer support to each other in a number of ways. Illums Bolighus is Scandinavia's leading design destination, and Epal gave us the chance to develop a fragrance in the region's fifth national language: Icelandic.

What are some of your favourite restaurants,
design destinations and hangouts?

Our office is just around the corner from Værnedamsvej, one of Copenhagen's cosiest streets, and it is hard to beat having a coffee or something to eat in one of the restaurants there, like Granola, Rist or Falernum. One neighbourhood we especially like is Kødbyen, the old meatpacking district, for the constant buzz of people and food. Basically, pretty much anywhere in Vesterbro is very *hyggelig*.

Snøhetta

This collaborative architectural practice, founded by Kjetil Trædal Thorsen and Craig Edward Dykers in 1987 and named for a Norwegian mountain, has expanded to include locations in Europe, the US, and beyond. The company exemplifies the architectonic style of Scandinavian housing and living, and has won numerous awards for projects that range from shop interiors to an underwater restaurant.

Snøhetta began as a collaboration between architects and landscape architects, exploring projects in which new structures work with the existing landscape, site and context. Today, the team consists of architects, landscape architects, interior designers, graphic and brand designers, researchers and artists. The company began to work internationally in the 1980s, and now has offices in Oslo, New York, San Francisco, Innsbruck, Adelaide and Stockholm. The New York office was set up when the firm was commissioned to design the 'Cultural Complex' at Ground Zero in 2004, and today has 50 employees. Smaller offices are opened when the company receives a commission in a new city (such as San Francisco, after securing the SFMoMA expansion project).

'We like to think that we translate ideas from the Nordic model into our projects. Everybody has a voice. We are open to ideas, and like the idea of giving something back to the public.'

Kjetil, where does the inspiration for each new project come from?

Every project is a new challenge, and each one has a programme, site, location and end users. The inspiration is different each time, from day to day, year to year. We have staff from over 30 countries, who all bring something different to the table. We like to think that we translate ideas from the Nordic model into our projects, and are inspired by everyday life in Scandinavia. Everybody has a voice. We are open to ideas, and like the idea of giving something back to the public. We follow our projects through from A to Z, which means that we work on construction sites. We prefer to work with the craftsmen in the country we work in and respect their traditions, but also challenge them to learn something new. It is very inspiring to use local materials and old techniques in a new way and in a new design context.

Inspiration can be found anywhere. I like to travel, and travelling in Scandinavia always offers something new to discover. I enjoy seeing new built projects and how they improve or disappoint over time. Visiting museums, conferences and exhibitions is essential to update and refresh ideas. Stockholm and Copenhagen have great personalities and a sense of metropolitan urbanity that is also reaching Oslo. Our work takes us to so many new and interesting places, and the people who live and work there are always inspiring.

What are some of the projects you're working on at the moment?

On my desk today is the '7th Room', a new room in the treetops at Treehotel (p. 250) in Harads, northern Sweden. Other projects include an underwater restaurant in southern Norway, a new lamp design in collaboration with Atelje Lyktan, a Swedish lighting company, and a public plaza at Stureplan in Stockholm. We have also collaborated with Bjarne Melgaard on *A House to Die In*, which was shown at the Institute of Contemporary Arts in London.

What does Nordic design mean to you?

Nordic design can seem a bit of a cliché to the rest of the world. It's important to remember that we are lucky to have a stable economy and are able to share common ideas about equality. We really appreciate the best of what the Nordic lifestyle has to offer, being close to the outdoors and taking care of it, and what we feel is the essence of design: use good materials and make it functional and beautiful in its own simple way.

'It is crucial to create a fun and playful
environment – for us, the people we work
with and the people who participate in our
events. If you don't have a good time at
work, you simply won't deliver your best.'

Space 10

Space 10, founded by Carla Cammilla Hjort and based in Copenhagen's former meatpacking district, brings together creatives with the aim of finding solutions to urban living while keeping *hygge* firmly at the forefront. The company also functions as Ikea's external innovation lab, redefining what it means to think outside the box.

The mission at Space 10 is to explore the future of urban living by identifying issues that will impact people on a global scale, and then coming up with solutions that will lead to a better, more sustainable way of living.

'We live in interesting times,' Carla notes. 'The world is improving on so many levels, but we are also facing challenges that, over the next decade or so, will result in a qualitatively different world. There will be around 8.3 billion people in 2030, and this, along with the consumption patterns of an expanding middle class, means that the demand for resources will grow substantially. It's estimated that within the next 15 years the planet will need 50 per cent more energy, 40 per cent more clean water and 35 per cent more food.'

Why do you believe it is important to create spaces that bring people together?

We are a small team, so co-creation is essential. We see ourselves as facilitators of the innovation process. There are so many inspiring and brilliant people out there, so why compete with them if we can join forces and work together? We enable people to improve the world by making use of their areas of expertise, in ways they are passionate about.

This approach also ensures fresh perspectives and experts in so many different fields. We would never have been able to deliver that diversity and creativity with a permanent in-house team. Imagine if Apple had to develop all of its apps by itself! Integrating different formats – workshops, talks, screenings, exhibitions, collaborations with students or reaching out to existing start-ups – is the best way to involve the community in the entire process.

Does hygge *have a part to play in the look or experience of the spaces you design?*

It is crucial to create a fun and playful environment – for us, the people we work with and the people who participate in our events. If you don't have a good time at work, you simply won't deliver your best. It's not just about *hygge*, it's also about Scandinavian values in general, including human rights, equality, dignity, democracy, trust, happiness and extending an overall humanity to others. We share these values and we always put people first. We want to help them thrive, to make life easier, better, richer, simpler, more sustainable, safer and more equal, playful and aesthetically pleasing. Together we can create a better life for everyone. It's the sum of many small initiatives that will eventually make a big impact.

I am not smart enough to predict the future. I find it more interesting to think about how we can influence and create the future we want, but I hope that we will experience more solidarity, equality, dignity and happiness across the globe, and that governments, companies and individuals will begin to think long term. I desperately hope that we are moving into an age where people not only look at what they buy, but also what they buy into.

Stilleben

Jelena Schou Nordentoft and Ditte Reckweg's beautifully curated shop on Niels Hemmingsens Gade in Copenhagen is a mecca of design. With their focus fixed on ceramics and new designers, this design duo spreads the message of Nordic living by creating everyday 'stilleben' (still life) stories, inspired by travels and a love of Danish design.

After meeting as 18-year-olds while studying ceramic design at the Royal Danish Academy of Fine Arts, Jelena Schou Nordentoft and Ditte Reckweg set up Stilleben in 2002. Over the next few years, and after receiving a lot of interest from abroad, the pair decided it was time to launch an online store, which they did in 2005.

'We are now able to give our customers different experiences, which is very important to us,' they explain. 'We began working on our own design collection about two years ago, and today the range includes accessories, scented candles and prints. We are also about to launch our own tableware collection, which is made at our own ceramics factory on the Danish island of Bornholm, off the southeast coast of Sweden.'

Jelena and Ditte, what is it about Scandinavian design that is so appealing?

For us, it's all about simplicity and unpretentiousness. We are influenced by the region's significant design tradition, our history and tradition of democracy, as well as the natural world around us. As Scandinavians, our need to create *hygge* is the reason why our homes are so important to us. Decorating them is a way of expressing who we are. The ultimate in *hygge* is to be at home, making pancakes on a rainy day! When we create a 'stilleben', we tell a story about who we are, what we like, perhaps even where we have been travelling.

BUTIKKEN FORTSÆ
PÅ 2. SAL

Where should visitors to Scandinavia go to experience great design?

The Danish Museum of Art and Design in Copenhagen is a must: they have a beautiful collection in an amazing building, and a garden with its own café. A great restaurant is Admiralgade 26, also in Copenhagen. Go for the sublime interior with its handcrafted furniture, as well as the fantastic food and wine.

Our favourite designers include ceramicists Malinda Reich, for her beautiful one-of-a-kind handcarved pieces, and Anders Arhøj, for his humorous, colourful, Japanese-inspired universe. Among our favourite

'Our homes are very important to us Scandinavians, and decorating them is a way of expressing who we are.'

artists are Sarah Becker, for her poetic works on paper, and Anne Nowak, for her irresistible spraypainted prints.

Stutterheim

Fashion label Stutterheim has been supplying stylish, functional outdoor gear to Stockholm-based Swedes since 2010. Since then the company has achieved cult status, collaborating with the likes of Jay Z, Dover Street Market and Barneys New York, as well as with lifestyle brands including Ouur, the company behind Kinfolk.

One rainy day while working as a copywriter at Saab, Alexander Stutterheim sat down with a coffee and watched the people outside hurrying past. Noting the ugly, functional raincoats, cheap umbrellas and newspapers clutched above heads, he realized that there was nowhere to find decent but still stylish outdoor gear. A few weeks later, his grandfather passed away, and while cleaning out his house in Arholma, Alexander stumbled upon his old raincoat. It was a classic fisherman's raincoat, a plain and heavy garment made from sturdy oilcloth.

Despite its humble origins, it looked cool, if a bit tent-like, and the idea of creating a new, more modern raincoat was born. Alexander had no experience in fashion, but decided to have a go at designing a raincoat. 'It started out as a kind of anti-depression winter project,' he says. He marked out the pattern on the kitchen floor, and brought the prototype to Borås, where the last textile factory in southern Sweden was based. The skills, craftsmanship and attention to detail of the workers convinced Alexander that the raincoats should be made there.

'From the start, I had a clear vision of what I wanted to create with Stutterheim,' Alexander says. He wanted to convey the message that it's fine to feel down at times, and to feel blue when the weather is bad, and that it's important to embrace that feeling, because it might lead to something good – which itself can be a catalyst for creativity. More than just making raincoats, Alexander wanted to say something important about life – a goal that has given the brand the authenticity for which it has become known and loved.

Superunion Architects

Founded in Oslo in 2012 by Vilhelm Christensen and Johanne Borthne, Superunion has been named by *Wallpaper** magazine as among the 20 best young practices in the world. Key to the company's ethos is the creation of good architectural spaces, regardless of budget or expensive materials – a very Nordic philosophy.

'What is Norwegian style? An excessive use of timber? A closeness to nature? For a long time, Norway's architectural style was seen in connection with the legacy of Sverre Fehn, but we have moved on.'

After meeting at the Oslo School of Architecture and Design as students, Vilhelm Christensen and Johanne Borthne both ended up working in Rotterdam (Vilhelm for OMA, and Johanne for Powerhouse Company). After several years in the Netherlands, they returned to Norway to set up Superunion.

'For us, architecture is the perfect combination of the pragmatic and the artistic,' says Johanne. 'You can go in many different directions – administrator, researcher, designer, teacher, writer, urban designer. I was interested in everything, and I'm happy to say that now, as a partner in Superunion, I can combine all of those roles.'

Current projects include a temporary food market/cultural venue in the Oslofjord, a gallery interior in Moss (a city near Oslo), and a public square and housing area on the west coast of Norway. The team is also planning a continuation of a research project begun in 2016, 'City of Dislocation', about the empty cultural buildings in Oslo.

'Frank Lloyd Wright once said to consider building a chicken house as important as building a cathedral,' she continues. 'I very much agree: any commission is potentially exciting. In the office we have always had a range of scales, from interiors and furniture to masterplans and public spaces.'

Johanne, what makes Nordic architecture different from that of other countries?

Nordic architecture is often defined as minimalist and robust, functional and local, but I think the current scene is richer and more complex. Firms work more internationally now, and there is more emphasis on creating public spaces. In a way, creating a public space is the least sustainable financial investment you can make. A building represents a physical value that you can sell, but a public space is like a gift you bestow to make the environment more pleasant – perhaps a sign of how fortunate we are in Scandinavia to be able to make these kind of investments.

Do you have a specific style in Norway that is different to other Nordic countries?

I don't believe that Superunion's style is particularly Norwegian, because we are inspired by so many different things. But what is Norwegian style? An excessive use of timber? A closeness to nature? A 'poorer' version of the design traditions of Denmark and Sweden? (Norway was one of the poorest countries in Europe until we struck oil in the late 1960s.) For a long time, Norway's architectural style was seen in connection with the legacy of the architect Sverre Fehn, but we have moved on.

On the one hand, architecture is used as a tool for creating identity and diversity (the Oslofjord is a prime example of this), while on the other, Norwegian architecture has always been very connected to nature. Norway doesn't have many big cities in comparison to the rest of Europe. We are still a country with a lot of countryside and a lot of space. Many buildings that are created

in natural environments are very simple and beautiful, but I see that there is still a lot of trial and error, or perhaps potential, when it comes to creating more urban architecture and public spaces. In our office, we are very open-minded when it comes to being inspired. Relating to context is a key factor in our projects. I look at style as something that constantly evolves and adapts to the context and programme. It is very liberating not to have a preferred style.

What does hygge *mean in Norway, and do you apply it when you design buildings?*

Hygge is very much a Scandinavian term. What creates *hygge* is very personal, but essentially when you have a space with a good atmosphere, where people feel comfortable and safe, you have *hygge*. As urban designers, we try to orchestrate a pleasing atmosphere by creating spaces with good sun conditions, which are sheltered from the wind and with places to sit. When designing buildings it's the same principle: we look at the potential of a site and the environment, and create the physical framework for *hygge*.

Which projects are you most proud of?

I'm proud of every project! Asker Square was special because it was our first win, and I still like the robustness and clarity of the design, even though it was never realized for financial reasons. Istanbul DPEC, another of our first projects, was a competition proposal. It was worked out entirely in a physical model, and was later picked up by Kanye West, who saw it online. We designed the first interior for Galleri Haaken, and I'm happy to see that, many years later, it still looks and works as intended. I'm also

proud of our self-initiated projects, including Arne Garborg Square in Oslo, where we used a model to show how to create a new public space and preserve the Y-block in the government quarter.

What are the current trends in Scandinavian architecture, and how do you see it developing?

It will be interesting to see what happens in the architecture and design schools, because students and courses tend to pick up on trends very quickly. When I was a student, the Dutch 'diagrammatic' method of architecture was very strong, but today students are more interested in how things are detailed. One trend is to react against what went before. This semester I'm involved with three different architecture schools (Oslo, Bergen and Copenhagen), and it will

be interesting to see how they differ. At the Oslo School of Architecture and Design, there is a move towards a modern architectural language, perhaps a reaction to the current tendency for every building to be something special. I'm also pleased to see that students are concerned with environmental and humanitarian issues.

Uh La La Ceramics

Ceramics produced in this part of the world are often inspired by nature and have a seductive, appealing quality. Julie Bonde Bülck, working from a studio in the Nørrebro area of Copenhagen, uses her favourite material, porcelain, to create a typically Scandinavian fusion of functionality and beauty.

Having graduated from the Royal Danish Academy of Fine Arts in 2008, and after working for a year at Royal Copenhagen, Julie decided to set up on her own, developing and producing her designs. Today she numbers Relæ (p. 152) and Royal Copenhagen among her clients and was chosen to take part in *Wallpaper** magazine's Handmade 2013.

'I started at an early age, around four or five years old, drawing houses,' she says. 'My father was a construction engineer and carpenter, and I grew up in a house that he designed and built. Aesthetics, quality of materials and standards of craftsmanship were always appreciated and essential in our home. I think my designs reflect my Scandinavian design heritage, as well as my personality: soft, subtle yet innovative.'

Julie, how do your designs fit in with the idea of Nordic living?

Nordic living is about feeling comfortable and being seduced by a certain atmosphere. My goal is to enable people to engage with that feeling when seeing my designs, whether in the studio or at an exhibition or in their own homes. I like to create objects that invite people to use and admire them, as well as the idea of creating something people will want to use and keep for many years – something that you get emotionally attached to when you see the shape and surfaces and colours.

You worked in Scotland for a time in the late 1990s. What was that experience like?

A friend from school, Ida, suggested that I stay with her aunt Lotte Glob, a ceramicist based in Scotland who had hosted many students over the years. At the time her studio was in the far north of the country, in a small village near Cape Wrath. It was great to follow the work of an artist, who worked with both one-of-a-kind items and functional designs. Some pieces were made for exhibitions, and others were sold at the studio shop. The people I met there were intrigued by artists working with crafts, perhaps more so than Danes would be. The first thing they would ask was if I thought I could make a living from it. I think this has changed now, because of the increased interest in craftsmanship, heritage and authenticity.

'One piece of
advice to people
who want to work
with ceramics: start
at an early age, apply
for internships at
studios and factories
to gain experience,
and, above all,
be patient!'

*Tell us about the neighbourhood around
your studio. Do you have favourite places
to go to?*

My studio is in Nørrebro, a colourful,
multicultural neighbourhood that attracts
plenty of creative young people. My favourite
places are all on Jægersborggade, a little
street with a village-like atmosphere, where
we all know each other. Many of the shops
collaborate with each other; I've worked
with Relæ, which serves their food on my
dinnerware. I like to go to Manfreds for the
cosy atmosphere and a glass of wine, and
Coffee Collective for the best coffee in town.

What was it like taking part in Wallpaper*
Handmade 2013?

Taking part in the exhibition was an
amazing experience. All of the designs
were made especially for the show, and
the level of design and craftsmanship was
the very best. Some of the designs were
extremely expensive to make. The exhibitors
demonstrated a skill that was on a par with
haute couture, and I was proud to be among
some of the world's best designers, including
Jaime Hayon and Karim Rashid.

*Are there any other designers who particularly
inspire you?*

I'm often inspired by restaurants and
fashion magazines, for colours and textures.
Among my favourite fashion designers are
Phoebe Philo and Christophe Lemaire, who
both create designs that are innovative and
minimalistic at the same time, which is
hard. And, of course, Jonathan Eve of Apple:
he knows how to connect with people's
emotions, with seductive shapes and details,
and innovative technology.

WIK Oslo

Costume designer-turned-ceramicist Ragnhild Wik
began her career as a design manager at the Norwegian
firm Porsgrunds Porselænsfabrik. But having left the
commercial world of production behind, Ragnhild now
makes her one-off creations at her studio in the centre
of historic Oslo. Her ceramics are sold at design stores
and galleries, as well as at her own gallery and shop.

Ragnhild originally trained as a costume designer at the École Supérieure des Arts et Techniques de la Mode in Paris, graduating in 1993. Later, she left the world of fashion to work as a design manager at Porsgrunds Porselænsfabrik, where she discovered her love of ceramics. In 2006, Ragnhild was one of the co-founders of a new commercial porcelain brand, Wik & Walsøe, and six years later, established her own workshop. In 2014 she severed ties with the company and began to work full time in her studio.

Over the next few years she learned by exploring different raw materials, from heavy Chamotte stoneware to the finest porcelain. 'Being open-minded and exploring new areas of interest will allow you to find inspiration in places you wouldn't normally expect to,' she says. 'I find inspiration everywhere around me, all the time. The Norwegian landscape is especially fascinating, with its dramatically different seasons. Our cultural heritage and fairy tales are also a big inspiration.'

Tell us about your studio. What is the building like?

My studio space is in a 200-year-old stable in the oldest part of Oslo. I sent out several requests and asked around the neighbourhood, and, luckily, I got a response from the owners of this charming old building. It was far too big for me, but

I just had to move in. I use the extra space to showcase my designs, both as a shop and exhibition space, and use my studio as a meeting place for family, friends and colleagues. It is like my second home now, with secondhand furniture and things I have collected over the years, all of which creates a cosy atmosphere, very much in the spirit of Nordic *hygge*.

What have been some of your greatest achievements?

I have very few private customers – some arts and craft galleries, but mostly design stores. I want to keep my creative freedom and work on a very small scale. All my pieces are one-offs, and I do not have collections and standard price lists, so my customers choose from the objects I make. I believe my greatest achievement is that I left commercial mass-production behind. I feel blessed that I have been able to achieve total creative freedom in my work. I really do enjoy learning new things every day, and I'm currently working on a wall art piece with several hundred handcarved pieces of paper porcelain. That should keep me busy!

'The Norwegian landscape is particularly fascinating, with its dramatically different seasons. Our cultural heritage and fairy tales are also a big inspiration for me.'

Food
&
Drink

Kristian Baumann

Restaurant 108

108

Although a mere stone's throw away from Noma, the atmosphere and dining experience at this restaurant are poles apart. Kristian Baumannead, head chef and co-owner (together with Noma's own René Redzepi), embraces the same ideals of foraging, fermentation and close collaboration with farmers, but with a price tag that is more accessible – and relaxed style to match.

A relative newcomer on the block (108 opened in 2016), the seed was planted about five years before, when Kristian Baumannead decided it was time to leave his position as sous chef at Relæ (p. 152) and open his own restaurant. Despite having neither investors nor money, Kristian was clear about what he wanted. Shortly afterwards, he began working as head chef at 1.th in Copenhagen and talking with René Redzepi about the possibility of opening a new restaurant.

The pair realized that they had similar ideas: Kristian wanted to have his own restaurant, and René wanted to open a new space while still being able to focus on Noma. René had spotted a building at Strandgade 108 some time earlier, and they decided to move ahead. Kristian returned to Noma, and spent a year working at all the stations again while planning his new venture. Noma was relocated to Japan for a period, but once back in Denmark, he began planning 108 full time. Kristian thought about every detail, from the napkin holders to drawing up the plan for the kitchen, with a huge amount of work achieved in a short space of time.

Kristian, how does your new restaurant differ from Noma?

They are two very different restaurants. At 108, we cater to a larger audience, there is music, we pour the first glass of wine but then leave you to it. We want people to relax and have fun. Some tables are very close, so you can end up sharing food or a bottle of wine. The menu is à la carte, with 10 individual dishes and three sharing platters. If you want, you can come with five friends and go through the entire menu with a bottle of champagne, or you can come with your kids and share a grilled monkfish. We want our guests to be able to choose what kind of night they want to have. You can also order as you go, it's up to you. Just walk in and have a glass of wine at the bar while you wait for a table.

You have achieved so much in such a short time. What do you think the future holds?

We call 108 a 'Copenhagen kitchen'. We find inspiration in all the knowledge that has developed in the city over the past decade, and are proud to be part of its dining scene. We have built the restaurant, like Noma, on foraging and working closely with our suppliers. Combine this with everything I have learned in my career and on my travels, and you get 108. So far, I think we are on the right path. I am excited to see what the future holds for us; it has been an incredible journey. We are very lucky to have a great team and to have been received with open arms.

CURED MACKEREL IN CELERY VINEGAR

CURED AND PICKLED MACKEREL
2 mackerel
salted green gooseberries
spruce wood oil
kelp salt flakes

Cut the mackerel into fillets and remove the bones. Cover with pine salt (see right), and leave for 1 hour at room temperature.

Mix equal parts celery vinegar with filtered water and heat to 38° C (100° F). Place the fish in vacuum bags, and add 50 ml (3½ tbsp) of the celery vinegar brine per fillet. Vacuum at full for 1½ hours at room temperature.

Remove the top layer of skin of the fish. Cut into triangles, and keep in an airtight container in the fridge.
To serve, place 6 triangles in a circle on a fridge-cold plate. On top of each triangle, add 1 tsp chopped salted gooseberries and a flake of kelp salt.

Finally, add a drizzle of spruce wood oil to the middle of the plate, and tilt it so that the oil is evenly distributed.

Note:
The mackerel should be no more than 500 g (1 lb), or the fish will be too tough. Keep in the fridge until you are ready to serve, as it will take only a minute or two for the fish to come to the right temperature.

PINE SALT
10 g (2 tsp) Guérande salt
15 g (1 tbsp) frozen pine shoots

Pound the pine shoots in a mortar and pestle until finely ground, then add the salt and pound again. Keep in an airtight container in the freezer.

Anders Schønnemann

With his exquisite eye for detail, food and lifestyle photographer Anders Schønnemann captures the essence of living the Nordic good life in his work. His photographs have been featured in books and magazines, and have garnered a large following on Instagram.

Having photographed everyone from Gordon Ramsay to René Redzepi, for clients that range from *Jamie* magazine to *Vanity Fair*, Anders Schønnemann remains remarkably modest about his work. 'I am fortunate to be a part of many different teams of extremely talented people,' he says. 'The creation of a beautiful photograph is, for me, the mark of a successful collaboration.'

And when it comes to what inspires him, Anders is equally modest. 'My approach to photographing interiors and food is all about the soft, natural daylight of Scandinavia,' he explains. 'I don't believe in creating the perfect image — what is perfect to me may not be the same to others, which is what makes photography so interesting. As a lifestyle photographer, I have been lucky enough to travel the world, experience new things and meet people who see life differently from me. That is my greatest inspiration.'

Anders, which restaurants or designers do you think particularly capture Scandinavia?

The most obvious restaurant is Noma, which I definitely think captures the essence of Nordic food and produce. But over the last three to five years, Copenhagen has seen a new range of small restaurants that produce wonderful Nordic food. Danish designers such as Hans J.

Wegner, Poul Kjærholm and Arne Jacobsen are recognized around the world for their designs, and at the moment there is such an interesting scene of both established and up-and-coming designers and architects, all of whom will no doubt keep Danish design on the map.

What recent projects or collaborations have you most enjoyed working on?

I recently worked on a cookbook called *Gone Fishing*, which was a very personal project as I collaborated with my friend Mikkel Karstad (p. 136). Many of the photographs capture what I feel to be the essence of *hygge*: mornings by the sea in that special light; the smell of a bonfire in the woods; good food and wine enjoyed outside during the long nights of summer.

Being able to combine work and friendship, and to create a book that people will enjoy for years to come, makes me both happy and proud. Having so many international clients also gives me the chance to travel the world, and to see places that I never dreamed I would. Sometimes I am able to bring my children, and it is wonderful to be able to share new experiences with them.

For those new to Nordic cooking, is there a particular recipe you would recommend?

I would always recommend indulging in a meal that includes lumpfish roe. The season for it is very short (four to six weeks, from the end of January to mid-March), but it is one of my favourite things to eat.

Fäviken

This remote restaurant is located in the small municipality of Åre, in northwestern Sweden, far away from the urban centre of New Nordic cuisine. Run by acclaimed chef Magnus Nilsson since 2008, it has achieved huge success, being named one of the world's 50 best restaurants in 2012, and among the top 10 the following year.

Having worked in several kitchens in Paris, including L'Astrance, Magnus Nilsson returned to Sweden with the intention of becoming a sommelier. Initially, he was hired to oversee the wine cellars at Fäviken, which at the time was no more than a local joint serving moose-fondue to the skiing community. But when the restaurant was unable to find a head chef, Magnus turned his attention to food.

The harsh climate, with its long, dark winters, would be a challenge for any chef, let alone one of international standards, but Magnus set to work, cutting down on corporate groups and large seatings to focus instead on a smaller, more intimate venue.

The plan worked, and Fäviken now has a long waiting list, something of an achievement given the remoteness of the location. Magnus built his team slowly, and with difficulty owing to the restaurant's location, but adhered to the tradition of achieving the highest quality possible. The restaurant is surrounded by 20,000 acres of farmland, which provides much of the game and root vegetables for the menu.

'During the summer and autumn we harvest what grows on the estate and prepare it using methods we have rediscovered from our rich culinary traditions, or that we have created through our own research,' Magnus explains.

He and his team had to find ever-more inventive ways of making the best use of the mountainous farmlands, working in tune with the seasons and the constant challenge of the weather and short supply and variety of the local produce. But with challenges came creativity, and the restaurant developed.

'We build up our stores ahead of the dark winter months,' says Magnus. 'We cure, salt, preserve, pickle and bottle. The hunting season starts after the harvest and is an important time, when we take full advantage of the bounty the mountains provide us with. By the time spring and summer return to Jämtland, the cupboard is bare and the cycle begins all over again.'

Being environmentally friendly and staying local are key to the philosophy that underpins Fäviken. 'We do things as they have always been done in Jämtland's mountain farms,' Magnus says. 'We follow the seasons and our traditions. We live alongside the community.'

Gastrologik

This innovative restaurant in Stockholm is run by Jacob Holmström and Anton Bjuhr. There is never a menu, as the two chefs work closely with their producers and decide in the morning what they will be cooking and serving that evening.

When Jacob Holmström and Anton Bjuhr founded their restaurant in 2011, in the Ostermalm district of Stockholm, their focus was firmly on the ingredients. Their aim is to 'surprise' guests, with as much effort put into sourcing ingredients as into cooking them. The pair knew from their school days that they wanted to set up a restaurant together, and eventually pooled their experience and resources to set up Gastrologik.

'For us, the important thing when choosing the ingredients is quality, rather than demand,' they say. 'Yellow onions are as important as truffles. Nature doesn't elevate them in terms of good or bad – people do. Because of that, respect and honesty are at the heart of what we do. It means that we can always honestly say that we are working with the best ingredients available on the day. This means that nobody knows what tonight's menu will include. It is always a question of the best possible ingredients available, what our suppliers can offer and the skills performed in the kitchen. This is why we do not provide a regular menu. Every guest is unique, as is every dish.'

Jacob and Anton, how important is your relationship with your suppliers?

We want to work as closely with nature and as regionally as possible, which is why we pick up our ingredients ourselves from our suppliers, from collecting milk from small farms in the area to picking herbs on our hands and knees at Rosendals Trädgård. This way we can better understand the work behind the produce, as well as gaining ideas and information from our suppliers. Running a restaurant of our own isn't a business, it's a way of life.

What plans do you have for the restaurant in the future?

We had originally considered running two separate restaurants, but with our philosophy, four hands are better than two. We complement each other, in that we are good in different areas but share the same vision and influences. Gastrologik is all about creating the ultimate food experience.

PERCH WITH SWEDISH FLAVOURS

1 large perch (about 1 kg, or 2 lbs)
10 sprigs of dill
1 onion
10 small new potatoes
500 ml (2 cups) sour whey
wild garlic flowers
chive flowers
anchovies (preferably Swedish
    anchovies, from Abbe Grebbestad)
butter

Fillet the perch and cut the backloins into 4 portions. Salt lightly, then set aside. Smoke the offcuts from the fish with juniper branches for a good 2 hours, then put them in a saucepan with cold water, a few sprigs of dill and an onion. Let simmer for 1 to 2 hours, then strain and reduce. Cold-smoke the perch fillets for 1 hour with the same juniper branches. Cook the potatoes in the whey, then cut into slices, brush with butter and set aside. Fry the fillets with butter, then dress with the remaining sprigs of dill and the chive flowers. Finish the sauce with browned butter.

SORREL ICE CREAM WITH CUCUMBER AND SPRUCE SHOOTS

SORREL ICE CREAM
200 g (1 cup) sugar
95 g (3¼ oz.) glucose powder
350 ml (1½ cups) water
150 ml (½ cup) sorrel juice
300 ml (1¼ cups) sour cream

Make a syrup with the sugar, glucose powder and water, and leave to cool. Mix the cooled syrup with the sorrel juice and sour cream. Freeze in Pacojet bowls.

GRANITA WITH SORREL
AND CUCUMBER
300 ml (1¼ cups) cucumber juice
300 ml (1¼ cups) sorrel juice
100 g (½ cup) sugar
wood sorrel
pine shoots

Mix all of the ingredients together and freeze, scraping through occasionally with a fork. Sprinkle on top of the sorrel ice cream, and top with a few leaves of wood sorrel and pine shoots.

Geranium

When Geranium received its third Michelin star in 2016, it was the first Danish restaurant to be so honoured (Norwegian restaurant Maaemo [p. 126] has also received three stars). Chef/owner Rasmus Kofoed, 2011 Bocuse d'Or winner, with his signature perfectionism and attention to detail, is the vision behind it.

Geranium's location on the 8th floor overlooking the Fælledparken, with views out towards Øresund, the sea between Sweden and Denmark, is hard to beat. Diners look out across Copenhagen's urban architecture and the city's many parks, while the open kitchen offers a view of the action, an artistic display of chefs working their magic. The light and airy dining room offers the minimalist Nordic approach to fine dining, an experience you won't find anywhere else on the planet.

Prior to setting up Geranium together with sommelier Søren Ledet in 2007, chef Rasmus Kofoed worked at the two-Michelin-starred restaurant Scholteshof in Stevoort, Belgium, and Hotel d'Angleterre in Copenhagen. He has won bronze, silver and gold at the prestigious Bocuse d'Or cooking competition in France, one of the only chefs to do so, and was featured in the 2011 documentary, *World's Best Chef*.

Geranium is a regular on the top 50 list of the world's best restaurants, and offers diners a menu that lists up to 20 dishes, which change according to the seasons. The emphasis is on exploring regional culinary treasures, such as wild herbs and flowers, as well the best local organic produce. Dining at the restaurant is an artistic exploration into Scandinavia's wild landscape, with some surprising twists to otherwise familiar dishes. Whatever you order, Geranium will whisk you away on a magical culinary journey.

JERUSALEM ARTICHOKE LEAVES

Serves 4

100 g (3½ oz.) Jerusalem artichokes, cooked
¼ tsp salt
100 ml (¼ cup) mayonnaise
3 tbsp walnut oil
rye vinegar, to taste

Peel the artichokes and vacuum-pack tightly, then boil in water until soft. Blend the now-soft artichokes and salt together until you have a smooth purée. Pass through a sieve and cool. Spread on a nonstick baking sheet and form into leaf-like shapes. Bake at 90° C (194° F) for 45 minutes, or until crispy. Mix the mayonnaise and walnut oil together, and serve with rye vinegar.

Kontrast

The industrial setting of the Oslo-based Kontrast is the realization of a longheld dream of chef Mikael Svensson. The restaurant, which received its first Michelin star in 2016, offers over a thousand different wines, and a changing six- or 10-course menu, according to the seasons.

Born and raised in Skåne, in southern Sweden, Mikael Svensson has cooked in restaurants since he was 16 years old. 'I always liked the vibe and feeling in the kitchen,' he explains. 'As the years went by and I became better and better, I climbed the career ladder until the time came when I wanted to create something on my own. I felt the need to be part of all the planning and decision-making that goes into creating a good restaurant experience. There was no job like this available, so I decided to do it on my own. It has always been a dream to have my own restaurant.'

Mikael, why are Scandinavian ingredients so important in your cooking?
My career began in the countryside in southern Sweden, where we didn't have fancy suppliers with ingredients from around the world. We got our duck from the neighbour, another farmer had eggs, and so on. I'm not limited to Scandinavian ingredients necessarily, but we always source our main ingredients from the farmers around us. We buy whole animals for meat, and visit the farmer ahead of time to see the animal and how it lives before we decide to buy it and put it on our menu. We try to use the whole animal in a respectful way.

Vegetables, herbs, berries and fruit are also better if they are picked when they are ripe and have a short transportation. So we try to source our ingredients as locally as possible. This forces us to change the menu with the micro-seasons, as well as the main seasons, ensuring that the menu is constantly evolving.

What is the location of your restaurant, and why did you choose it?

We are located in the centre of Oslo, right next to a park and a food market, near the lively neighbourhood of Grünerløkka and a short distance from Karl-Johans Gate and the Royal Palace. We have the option of having a rooftop garden, as well as our own beehive, on top of the food market, and we can go urban-foraging in the park.

How is Kontrast different from other Nordic restaurants, many of which also have Michelin stars?

I hope and believe we have our own style, and that guests can appreciate the differences when they are dining at Kontrast. Receiving the Michelin star has given us a lot of extra attention within Norway, as well as outside of the country. The fact that we then get more guests opens up the opportunity of hiring more staff and expanding the business, which will hopefully lead to a better product and, in the end, a better restaurant.

LIGHTLY SALTED SCALLOPS WITH RAW SWEET PEAS AND NASTURTIUMS

Serves 4

SCALLOPS
4 large, fresh scallops
sea salt

Open and rinse the scallops, pat dry and lightly salt on both sides. Place on a dry cloth (changing the cloth often), and keep in the fridge for 2 days to mature the flavour.

SCALLOP-ROE EMULSION
50 ml (3½ tbsp) organic tamari soy sauce
2 organic egg yolks
horseradish, grated, to taste
50 ml (3½ tbsp) water
100 g (¾ cup) blanched scallop roes
500 ml (2 cups) ice-cold vegetable oil

Beat the soy sauce, egg yolks, horseradish, water and scallop roes until smooth, then stir in the oil gently to form an emulsion. Salt to taste, then sieve through muslin.

PEA SALAD
200 g (1⅓ cups) organic peas in the pod
salt
1 tbsp organic cold-pressed rapeseed oil
200 g (1⅓ cups) organic sugarsnap peas
1 bunch of nasturtiums

Split the pea pods, and separate the larger peas from the smaller ones. Reserve the small peas. Blanch the larger peas for 30 seconds, then plunge into ice water. Peel the now-blanched peas, and keep them to one side with the raw ones. Finely slice the sugarsnaps and blanch in salted water for 30 seconds. Drain, add the peas, and rapeseed oil and salt to taste.

Process the pea pods in a juicer. Set aside 12 nasturtium leaves for garnishing the plate, and press the rest through a juicer – leaf, stem and all. Add a little nasturtium juice and salt to taste; it should be sweet with a bit of spice.

Slice the scallops and mix with the pea salad. At the bottom of a deep plate, put a generous dollop of the emulsion. Cover with the pea and scallop salad, then garnish with the nasturtium leaves and flowers, and serve.

Maaemo

With a name that comes from an old Norse word meaning 'Mother Earth', Maaemo is located in the Bjørvika area of Oslo and headed up by chef/co-owner Esben Holmboe Bang. The restaurant is committed to the Norwegian tradition of using local ingredients in season.

Originally from Copenhagen, Esben Holmboe Bang arrived in Oslo a decade ago with his Norwegian wife, Kaja. During that time, the city has experienced a dramatic transformation as one of the fastest-growing in Europe. Esben set up Maaemo in 2012 and the restaurant received two Michelin stars the same year – the first time a Nordic restaurant has done so in its first mention in the guide. In 2016 Maaemo and Copenhagen-based Geranium (p. 116) were each awarded three stars, the first Nordic restaurants to be so honoured. Maaemo uses organic, biodynamic or wild produce.

'The idea was to forge a unique Norwegian identity that was part gastronomical, part cultural,' Esben explains. 'It wasn't easy at first, as most fine-dining restaurants in Norway tended to look to France for inspiration, while we focus solely on Norwegian produce. But now people have a clear idea of what we stand for, and are very supportive of our efforts to build on Norway's rich culinary heritage. It's been tremendously satisfying to think that we have played a part in changing the country's culinary landscape for the better.'

Esben, why is using Norwegian ingredients so important in your cooking?

Norwegian food places a lot of emphasis on preserving the produce in the growing season. We have very harsh winters and the growing season is only three to four months long, so it is very important that we make sure we are stocked up for winter. It's not easy: we have to plan and we have to fight for it.

Why did you choose the Bjørvika district of Oslo as the location for Maaemo?

The area is relatively new, just like Maaemo. I wanted the restaurant to be in a new area without any prejudice. A lot of ambitious restaurants opened in the western part of town, so we wanted to do something different. The restaurant is very central, close to the railroad station and Bjørvika, the new financial district. We are a Norwegian restaurant, not a Nordic restaurant.

Oslo is changing fast, and the driving force of creativity lies with the younger generation. Compared to our Scandinavian neighbours, I feel that Oslo's creative identity is stronger as it develops at a slower pace. There's a real buzz to the city now.

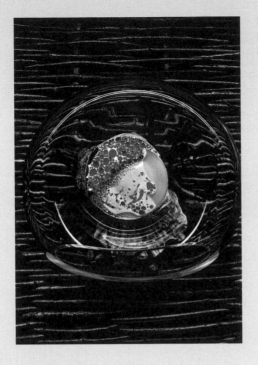

MUSSEL GEL
420 ml (1¾ cups) mussel stock
110 ml (½ cup) oyster liquor
4 g (1 tsp) agar

Place the stock and oyster liquor in a pot, then whisk in the agar. Bring to the boil, still whisking, and then turn down to a simmer. Continue to whisk for 1 minute. Strain quickly through muslin into a sealable funnel. Spread evenly over two very flat baking sheets, and lightly blowtorch the bubbles. Leave to cool, then place in the fridge. When the gel has cooled and set, remove and cut with a 7-cm (3-in.) round cutter. Place the gel back on the tray and keep refrigerated.

DILL OIL
600 ml (2½ cups) rapeseed oil
200 g (7 oz.) dill

Place the oil and dill in a Thermomix. Set at 50° C (122° F), speed 6, for 15 minutes. Strain through muslin and let settle. Pour into a vacuum bag, leaving the water behind. Vacuum, then freeze if needed for later use.

MUSSEL CREAM
500 ml (2 cups) mussel stock
500 ml (2 cups) double cream
salt, to taste
dill oil

Place the mussel stock and cream into a pot. Bring to the boil, then turn down to a simmer and reduce by half. When the liquid is reduced, cool over an ice bath, stirring continuously, to keep it from getting lumpy. Refrigerate when cool. To serve, heat, season with salt and – at the last second – split with dill oil.

EMULSION OF RAW OYSTERS WITH A WARM SAUCE OF MUSSELS AND DILL

MUSSEL STOCK
3 kg (6½ lbs) mussels
700 ml (3 cups) good white wine

Warm the mussels in cold water and leave to soak for 5 minutes, then strain. Put the wine in a pan that has a lid, bring to the boil and place the mussels inside. Cover, and bring back to the boil. When the mussels have opened, strain the stock through muslin. Chill over an ice bath, and refrigerate.

Mielcke & Hurtigkarl

Executive chef and partner Jakob Mielcke of Mielcke & Hurtigkarl, located in the garden of the Royal Danish Horticultural Society in Frederiksberg, is a well-known name in the Danish culinary world. Self-taught, he has worked with the likes of Pierre Gagnaire, in both London and Paris, and was recently named one of the 100 most creative chefs in the world.

Business partner Jan Hurtigkarl's previous restaurants include Les Etoiles in Copenhagen and Jan Hurtigkarl & Co. in Ålsgårde. 'The principal idea behind the restaurant was to invite the garden inside,' Jakob explains. 'Ninety per cent of our ingredients are from our garden or from the farms we work with. The remainder is made up from a few ingredients, mainly from Asia, which have become part of our food DNA.'

When it came to decorating the restaurant, he says, 'I wanted more green, more *hygge*. So I roped in a team of friends from different fields: fashion designer Henrik Vibskov, textile designer Margrethe Odgaard, set designer Simon Holk Witzansky and lighting designer Mads Vegas. I could also have paid the same company that designed Noma and Geranium (p. 116), but that would have been the most uninspired choice I could have made. Instead, we created a story. So far, we haven't regretted a thing.'

Jakob, what are your goals and aspirations for the restaurant?

Instead of opening other restaurants and dividing my time and attention between different kitchens, I want to focus on the future of this restaurant and my cooking. I have a lot of time ahead of me, and many new things to explore. That's why we call our menu a metamorphosis.

Does hygge *have any part to play in your restaurant or choice of ingredients?*

I wouldn't necessarily call it '*hygge*', but sustainability is a very important component of everything we do. This is also carried through in our staff. We can't be a restaurant that sustains people if we are not self-sustaining, and the same goes for our produce. We need it to be good, but in itself this is not enough. It needs to be grown slowly, and balanced. The chain from crop to table must be one that is sustainable, in all its forms.

What are some favourite ingredients that you like to use at the restaurant?

We are very fortunate in Denmark to have four distinct seasons. These are key to defining ourselves, both in terms of our personality and our ingredients and food. Many people from warmer climates fear the colder seasons, but gastronomically they are magnificent. Our vegetables, berries and fruits may be fewer, with a shorter season, but they also have a more distinctive taste. Because vegetables are so scarce in winter, this forces us to be much more creative.

Mikkel Karstad

Danish chef and food stylist Mikkel Karstad is the embodiment of the international fascination with the New Nordic cuisine, and Scandinavian food in general. A student of the acclaimed chef Claus Meyer, he is also the author of several cookbooks, including *Gone Fishing* (see also Anders Schønnemann; p. 102) and *Spis*.

Although born and raised in Copenhagen, Mikkel Karstad spent much of his childhood on the island of Tåsinge, where his grandmother had a garden laden with vegetables, fruit and berries, and taught him the importance of using produce in season. Mikkel would often go hunting and fishing with his uncle, who taught him how to skin deer and pluck the feathers off pheasants.

'My childhood was a good mix of the city and the countryside, which is reflected in my food,' he says. 'I always try to cook with what is in season. In the spring, the first wild herbs, edible flowers, asparagus and new potatoes begin to appear, followed by berries, peas, carrots, beans and mushrooms in the summer. In the autumn, I focus on apples, pears, root vegetables and cabbage, which can also be used throughout the winter. It makes sense to follow the old ways of doing things. My grandmother would find it very amusing that simple processes – smoking, salting, fermenting – have become so trendy!'

Mikkel, do you have any favourite ingredients that you return to again and again?

I've always been very interested in foraging, fishing and hunting, but it became a very big part of my work when I began working for Claus Meyer, over a decade ago. Whatever is in season, at that moment, is what I love best, but I really enjoy cooking vegetables and seafood. Danish squid is one of my favourites.

Does the Scandinavian concept of hygge *apply to your cooking?*

A good meal consists of many things. Of course, it is important that the food is good, but equally important are the company you eat with and atmosphere you eat in. I once heard about a study in which people were asked what their best meal was, and most could not remember what they ate, but they could remember exactly whom they had eaten it with. So *hygge* really is an essential part of any meal.

*Is your perfect meal traditionally
Scandinavian, or would you add your
own style?*

A favourite is summer cabbage, which we
have a lot of. Cabbage used to be considered
a poor man's food, but now it is very popular.
I would cook it on a hot grill and serve it with
some steamed mussels, wild herbs and butter:
basic, simple and local. Because you eat with
your eyes first, how food is presented is very
important. For me, that means as simply and
honestly as possible, so that the ingredients
are able to speak for themselves. I often
present meals on Nordic stoneware and
ceramic plates. I have no real collaboration
with Danish potters, I just think that they are
very well suited to the way I think and cook.

*How do you structure your day-to-day life
as an independent chef and food stylist?*

Days are rarely the same, but most
begin with getting the children up and off
to school and then leaving for a job. It all
depends on whether I'm styling food for
an advertisement or cooking for an event.
But one thing I always do – rain or shine, all
year round – is go for a swim in the ocean,
whether early in the morning or late at night.
It gives me a quiet space in which to relax and
escape from a hectic schedule with work and
four children.

SALTED BLACKCURRANTS

500 g (1 lb) fresh or frozen blackcurrants
10 g (2 tsp) salt

Put the berries and salt into an empty jam
jar and shake. Leave the jar, uncovered, for
4–5 days, until the berries start to ferment.
Stir once a day, but otherwise leave it alone.
Once the 4–5 days are up, put on the lid and
leave in the fridge or in a cold place.

GRILLED MACKEREL WITH SALTED BLACKCURRANTS AND CHIOGGIA BEETS

2 whole mackerel (or 4 fillets)
4 new Chioggia beets
½ tbsp good olive oil, plus more
   for the dressing
10 sprigs of thyme
1 tbsp salted blackcurrants
sea salt
freshly ground pepper

Check the fish for bones, or get your fishmonger to remove them. Cover with a bit of olive oil, salt and thyme, and leave to marinate for 10 minutes.

Wash the beets and cut them into thin slices on a mandolin, then leave to soak in a bowl of cold water.

For the dressing, stir the salted blackcurrants (opposite) and a bit of their liquid into some olive oil.

Grill the whole fish or fillets on a hot grill, skin side down for 2 minutes, until crisp and golden. Turn over and grill for a further 30 seconds. You want the fish to stay tender.

Take the mackerel off the grill and serve with thin slices of Chioggia beets and the salted blackcurrants. Sprinkle some thyme and sea salt on top.

Mikkeller

When it comes to having a *hyggelig* time, one of the essentials is a good drink. Brewing in Denmark is often associated with large producers, such as Carlsberg, but there are also many microbreweries. One of these is Mikkeller, co-founded by Mikkel Borg Bjergsø, which now sends its beer around the world.

Mikkel Borg Bjergsø's interest in beer began when he was a student in Copenhagen, working at a local café that imported beer from Belgium and the US. Although Danish beer was synonymous with large producers (like Carlsberg) at the time, a few microbreweries had also popped up in the city. After coming across, as he recalls, 'a really good IPA' from the Brøckhouse brewery in Hillerød, Mikkel began reading and experimenting in the kitchen with his friend and future business partner, Kristian Keller.

In 2006 Mikkel and Kristian received top ratings from RateBeer.com for their oat stout 'Beer Geek Breakfast', which led to several US distributors getting in touch. Four years later, they opened their first bar on Viktoriagade. The pair's ambition was to open a bar for novices and aficionados alike that was sophisticated yet welcoming, without the usual flat-screen television and oversized furniture. Meanwhile Keith Shore, their art director, was hard at work developing the bar's visual identity.

Mikkel, where do you find inspiration, and how does hygge *fit into your business?*

I get inspiration from travelling around the world and from people I collaborate with. I've always been adventurous when it comes to food and drink, and taste as many different things as possible. *Hygge* is a lifestyle, but essentially it's all about having a good time together, in pleasant surroundings with great people and delicious things to eat and drink.

Do you have any plans for further expansion, or for more types of beer?

We have lots of plans and projects going on. We don't sit still, and are constantly brewing new beer. In 2016, we opened up new places in Tórshavn in the Faroe Islands, Los Angeles, Taipei and Berlin.

ØsterGRO

This rooftop plantation in Copenhagen sums up the Scandinavian approach to life, with its focus on ease and togetherness, a down-to-earth attitude and an emphasis on simple ingredients – a philosophy echoed by many of today's top Nordic chefs.

A former wasteland in the heart of Copenhagen has been transformed into an organic farm, with workshops and classes for children that teach them about ecological and urban farming, as well as a restaurant in the greenhouse, with a waiting list from the start of spring to the end of summer. The founders – Livia Urban Swart Haaland, Kristian Skaarup and Sofie Brincker – met while setting up Ottilia's Garden in Vesterbro in 2013. To realize her dream of setting up a community garden, Livia abandoned an architecture degree to study ecological farming, followed by an internship at Brooklyn Grange, a rooftop farm in New York.

'One day in 2014, in early spring, we transported 110 tons of earth onto the roof of an old car-auction building, which had been prepared with a proper surface and edges by apprentices from Copenhagen Technical College,' Livia says. 'The entire site was reorganized in just one weekend with the help of over 100 wonderful neighbours and volunteers. With a decent quantity of compost, we planted both seeds and ideas,

which eventually became ØsterGRO. We now have a vegetable patch, a greenhouse, chickens, bees, rabbits, a composting area and an outdoor kitchen.'

The rooftop is looked after by two of the founders, the staff and the dedicated members and volunteers who want to take part. In return, they receive vegetables, eggs and honey. The vision for ØsterGRO is not to suggest that cities must be self-sufficient and grow all their food on rooftops, but to create a link between town and country. 'The increasing urbanization of our neighbourhoods has contributed to the loss of basic knowledge of how food is grown and produced,' say its founders.

Sustainability is key to their vision for ØsterGRO, along with communication and creating shared experiences. They have a genuine desire to make the city greener, with an increased focus on organic food, leading to richer taste experiences and more diverse communities around local food. ØsterGRO is all about sharing knowledge, and providing a green oasis in the heart of the city, inspiring its residents to lead a more sustainable life.

Relæ

Located in the Nørrebro area of Copenhagen, Relæ was
founded in 2010 by Christian Puglisi and Kim Rossen.
The pair have racked up an impressive number of
achievements in a short space of time: they have received
a Michelin star, been featured in the *Nordic Guide 2016*
and been named the world's most sustainable restaurant.

When Christian Puglisi decided to leave his position as sous chef at Noma, he wanted to create a restaurant where fine dining and an informal, relaxed atmosphere went hand in hand. Together with his business partner Kim Rossen, another Noma alum, Christian wanted to find ways of paring back as much as possible, to keep prices low. In keeping with this populist approach, the duo chose to locate their restaurant in the urban, somewhat gritty, bustling neighbourhood of Nørrebro in Copenhagen.

'Fine dining leaves an odd taste in my mouth,' Christian says. 'The hordes of waiters, the white tablecloths, chandeliers, and so on. That's not what I'm looking for when I dine myself. Honesty is the key, and Relæ is our own, honest version of a fine-dining experience. The district of Nørrebro is where my heart beats. When we opened Relæ, drug dealers were practically standing outside the front door. But things are beginning to improve, and it's starting to look like the kind of place we initially had in mind for our restaurant. We have been a part of the local movement to change the street into a group of independent, creative businesses.'

Christian, why is using local produce so important to your cooking?

Freshness and a very close relationship to the producers is a driving force in our cooking, so getting ingredients locally makes sense – along with the obvious ethical reasons, such as food miles and using only seasonal ingredients. It also allows us to have circular processes, like giving food scraps to feed the hens of the people we get our eggs from. Since opening Relæ, we have insisted on being a restaurant where innovative

gastronomy and low prices are not at odds with each other. This focus has required a development of carefully prepared daily routines and smart solutions.

What makes your restaurant stand out from the rest of the crowd on the New Nordic scene?

Our cut-to-the-bone concept is still quite unique, considering our Michelin star and rating as the 40th best restaurant in the world, as well as the fact that we are extremely serious in our approach to running a sustainable business. From the start, we thought creatively. How do we recycle? What do we save? Where do we look for synergy? From that point, the step towards an ethical, uncompromising approach to everything we do has fallen into place. We're not deliberately incorporating the concept of *hygge*, but some might argue that our restaurant's vibe is Nordic cool in that sense.

TURNIPS, CHERVIL AND HORSERADISH

Serves 6

THICK BUTTER EMULSION
250 g (9 oz.) unsalted butter, cut into cubes
250 ml (1 cup) boiling water
1 tsp xanthan gum

Combine the butter, boiling water and xanthan gum in a food processor, and process until emulsified, approximately 2 minutes. (Note: this will make more than you need for the recipe.)

REHYDRATED DEHYDRATED TURNIPS
2 kg (4½ lbs) turnips, peeled and trimmed
1 shallot, diced
1 bunch chervil, chopped
25 g (2 tbsp) unsalted butter, cut into cubes
lemon juice, freshly squeezed
salt

Slice the turnips into 2 cm (1 in.)-wide pieces, and place the slices in a single layer in a dehydrator. Dry at 65° C (150° F). When completely dried, transfer to a large bowl, add enough warm water to cover, and soak for 2 hours. Drain, and gently squeeze-dry with your hands. Slice into 1-cm (½-in.) strips.

Blanch the turnip strips in boiling salted water until al dente, 1 to 2 minutes. Drain, then transfer to a saucepan, and add the butter emulsion, shallot and chervil. Stir over medium-high heat until thoroughly blended. Add the butter and stir until emulsified, then season with lemon juice and salt.

TO SERVE
1 horseradish, peeled
12 g (4 tsp) black mustard seeds,
    toasted and slightly crushed

For each serving, place 3 large spoonfuls of turnips on the top quarter of the plate, in a flat layer. Using a small knife, slice off 8 or 9 pieces of horseradish and place them on top of the turnips. Sprinkle with the mustard seeds.

Studio

This Michelin-starred restaurant is located right in the centre of Copenhagen, by the 17th-century waterfront of Nyhavn, in an Art Deco building designed by Danish architect Kristoffer Nyrop Varming in the 1930s. At the helm is Claus Meyer, co-founder of Noma, who is often cited as the founding father of the New Nordic cuisine.

Head chef Torsten Vildgaard, who spent eight years at Noma as sous chef and head of research and development, earned Studio a Michelin star within five months of opening in 2013. Torsten and his team use local produce for their dishes, which derive mainly from Danish cuisine, although they also look for inspiration from the food and cooking of France and Japan. The restaurant's juice menu comprises Danish fruit and vegetables, pressed by the staff in the kitchen, 'which gives you just that extra level of Danish'.

'My philosophy and motto is always to keep testing,' he says. 'I want to extract the best parts of all sorts of ingredients and make them play together in a unique and powerful way. I'm always challenging myself to try new ways of cooking and new ingredients, and to make the experience amazing for every guest who comes through the door.'

Torsten, one of your entrées is served from a vase of flowers. Where does this creativity come from?

My staff and I are always working to improve in all aspects of the dining experience. Sometimes it doesn't work, but we learn from our mistakes and come back stronger. Hopefully, our efforts will take the restaurant to the next level.

What sort of role does hygge *play in the restaurant and in the food you serve?*

We have tried to make the restaurant as cosy and *hyggelig* as possible, as well as providing an internationally appealing atmosphere that is suitable for a meal of a certain standard. The experience of dining at Studio must be wonderful for our guests, and each member of staff works hard to make it memorable and filled with *hygge*, from the moment guests enter the door until they have finished their coffee. We have an open kitchen, which gives our patrons the chance to observe and understand the complexity and professionalism needed to make the dishes we create.

How do the seasons affect your choice of produce? And what are some of your favourite ingredients?

Each season has something unique to offer. My mood depends on the season, and this is reflected through the dishes we serve in terms of expression and colour. I love all ingredients when they are at their best – especially truffle, which can be used all year round.

RAW NORWEGIAN SCALLOPS WITH WHITECURRANT JUICE

Season some very fresh, preferably Norwegian scallops with salt and brown sugar, and keep in the fridge overnight. The next day, cut each one into 3 slices.

Combine 100 ml (½ cup) whitecurrant juice, 70 ml (4½ tbsp) water, sugar syrup (to 10 brix) and dill oil, before macerating with 5 g (1 tsp) chamomile buds.

Peel 4 large Jerusalem artichokes to produce 40 g (1½ oz.), and vac-pack in hazelnut oil. Steam for 35 minutes at 100° C (210° F), or until al dente. Plunge into ice water to cool, then cut into 1 cm (½ in.)-thick slices and place in a container lined with greaseproof paper.

Top with 3 halved blackberries, 2 raspberries that have been opened up and grilled, 5 blackcurrants, 2 halved red gooseberries, 1 stalk of whitecurrants, and apple vinegar from a spray bottle.

Garnish with the following herbs:
2 tergetis leaves
1 sprig of dill
3 small lovage leaves
1 lemon balm leaf
2 sprigs of lemon verbena
5 green coriander seeds
2 coriander flowers

Velo Coffee

Coffee lover Chad Ellingson from Portland, Oregon, moved to Stockholm in 2010 to pursue his passion for Scandinavian coffee roasters. He set up Velo Coffee, operating at first from an old secondhand bike, and now provides *fika* to visitors to Stockholm's weekend food market.

Chad Ellingson has been interested in coffee for as long as he can remember, but his passion really took off after he moved to Sweden in 2010, and was introduced to the typically Scandinavian flavours: intensely acidic and often citrusy. Once hooked, Chad bought a secondhand cargo bike from a day-care centre in Amsterdam and built a box to serve coffee from in a friend's workshop in his hometown of Portland, Oregon. Once the bike was built, he got in touch with Drop Coffee in Stockholm, who have provided essential support from the start.

Chad, why do you think Scandinavians are so much more aware of coffee quality than before?
Exposure to the world of speciality coffee has undoubtedly grown in Scandinavia. We are lucky to have green coffee buyers, such as Oslo-based Nordic Approach, collaborating with producers and bringing quality green coffees back to Scandinavia. Once the coffee is here, there are many wonderful, talented coffee roasters in the region. More people having the opportunity to try speciality coffee in their hometowns leads to more curiosity and awareness about quality coffees.

My ideal cup of coffee is served black, brewed and enjoyed with the person who roasted it. And if we're talking an *ideal* situation, have the person who farmed the coffee there, as well. Producer, roaster and consumer, all sharing coffee together: this is perfection.

What would you say is the best way to enjoy coffee in Sweden?
In Stockholm, we '*fika*': have coffee with a sandwich or pastry. It tends to be a very cosy affair. I prefer to brew and drink my coffee outdoors. Our favourite place to brew and serve is at Stockholm's weekend food market, Hornstulls Marknad: great food, secondhand clothes and, of course, coffee.

KANELBULLAR

Makes 25

35 g (1¼ oz.) yeast
100 g (½ cup) sugar
300 ml (1¼ cup) milk
1 egg
120 g (4¼ oz.) butter
1 tsp salt
1 tbsp ground cinnamon
750 g (6 cups) flour

FILLING
100 g (3½ oz.) butter
50 g (¼ cup) sugar
2 tbsp cinnamon

GLAZE
1 egg
2 tbsp water
Swedish pearl sugar

Preheat the oven to 220° C (425° F). Crumble the yeast in a bowl and stir in a few tbsp of milk. Melt the butter and pour the milk on top. Add the rest of the ingredients, and knead the dough in a mixer (with the dough hook attached) for 10–15 minutes. Cover the dough, and allow to rise at room temperature for 30 minutes.

Once it's risen, roll the dough out to about 3 mm (⅛ in.) thick and 30 cm (12 in.) wide, then spread the butter on top. Mix together the sugar and cinnamon, and sprinkle over the dough. Roll out lengthways, and cut into 25 slices. Put the slices with the cut edge facing up in paper cups, and then place on a baking sheet. Cover with a tea towel, and leave to rise for about an hour, or until the buns have doubled in size.

Beat together the egg and water. Brush this mixture on the buns, and sprinkle with pearl sugar. Bake in the oven for 5–6 minutes, then leave to cool on a rack.

fika

Kanelbullar

Art
&
Artists

Andreas Emenius

The creative output of Swedish artist Andreas Emenius, a graduate of Central Saint Martins in London and now based in Copenhagen, is varied and prolific. Among his projects are works on canvas, videos, installations and live performances. He is the curator and co-founder of Nordic Contemporary, a platform for contemporary Scandinavian artists, located in a 160m² (1,722 sq ft) empty apartment near the Place de la République, in Paris.

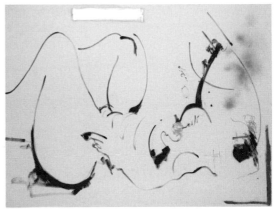

Andreas Emenius has also collaborated with Danish fashion designer Henrik Vibskov. After graduating from Central Saint Martins in 2000, they launched *The Fringe Projects* seven years later. Currently in its tenth instalment, the series includes works in the form of installations, performances, videos and self-portraits, exploring illusion, surface and movement, and has been exhibited at the Zeeuws Museum in Middelburg, Netherlands. Another project, *Circular Series*, focused on the role of a circle to clarify or visually glue, linking projects to the same universe, and explored the issue of identity and a person's place in the world.

A solo exhibition of Andreas's work was held at the Viborg Kunsthal in Denmark, in 2017, and he is also at work on a video collaboration with Danish music producer Trentemøller, co-directed by Åsa Riton. This latest project is a complete audiovisual experience, incorporating video projections, paintings, sculptures, sound and performance, and was shown in 2017, in cities including Los Angeles, Paris and Copenhagen.

Andreas, now that you have relocated to Denmark from Sweden, how do you find working in both countries?

Going back and forth between Sweden and Denmark and working in different studios seems to create a dynamic that works better for me. I also lecture at the Royal Danish Academy of Fine Arts, School of Design. Teaching, for me, is a conversation not only about looking at clear images, but also about what a picture really is, since it can be so many things, and not necessarily what the other person might think it means.

What kinds of projects are you working on at the moment?

Over the last few years, I have been studying physical movement and how to capture it in different ways by using painting, sculpture and the moving image. I am especially interested in kinetic phenomena, and how they appear to us and help shape our perception of an object or situation.

Birgitte Hjort Sørensen

One of the familiar faces of the Scandinavian television dramas that are so popular at the moment is actress Birgitte Hjort Sørensen. Her breakthrough role was in the Danish political drama *Borgen*, but she has also appeared in *Vinyl*, directed by Martin Scorsese, and as Karsi in *Game of Thrones*. In 2016, she appeared on Broadway in *Les Liaisons Dangereuse*s.

Growing up in the suburbs of Copenhagen, Birgitte had, she says, 'a very typical Danish childhood'. As a child, she loved playing 'dress up', putting on shows for her parents, and participating in the annual school play. After a six-month introductory course to acting, Birgitte entered the Danish National School of Performing Arts.

'I thought I would go straight to the Royal Danish Theatre and do lots of Shakespeare,' she says. 'My journey became very different when I got one of the lead roles in *Borgen*. By the time the show ended after three years, it had received a lot of international attention and I felt it was a good opportunity for me to pursue work abroad.'

Of her home country, she says: 'Each job offers its own challenges and opportunities, but playing Roxie Hart in *Chicago* in the West End just six months after graduating from drama school was very special. It was the first time I realized that we have something to offer in Denmark that is different from the countries we look up to. There were at least a thousand girls in London at the time with more training in musical theatre than me, but I realized that they liked the way I interpreted the role. We have a tendency in Denmark to think of ourselves as smaller and not as significant as the UK or the US, but this experience taught me that we have other qualities that are equally as valuable.'

Birgitte, how would you explain life in the Nordic countries to people who live elsewhere?

We have a pretty good balance between work and home life in Scandinavia. Most people don't have to face a long commute every day, and there's plenty of coastline, so the sea is never very far away. It's also fairly flat and with a lot of forests, so even in Copenhagen you feel pretty close to the countryside. Although I would love to live in a place where a nice, warm summer was guaranteed, I love the change of seasons. When the days get shorter, there's nothing better than curling up inside with candles and a cup of tea. We tend to go to each other's houses more, while it's more common in London and New York, say, to go out. We still go out, but I will just as often go to a friend's house as to a bar.

How do you think the Nordic lifestyle has played into the dramas we see on television?

Our long tradition in Scandinavia of good drama has had a huge influence on the way we do TV, which perhaps offers a more realistic, less glamorous view into the lives of the characters. Since we don't have the big Hollywood budgets, we focus instead on strong, character-driven stories.

There is a great feeling of safety, support and trust in our society. Yes, we pay high taxes, but with that comes free education and health care. When you visit other countries where that isn't the case, you realize how valuable it is. *Uhygge* in film and TV has a lot to do with our weather, as well as the subject matter. Crime, betrayal and power struggles aren't pleasant subjects perhaps, but they do make for great drama.

Cecilie Harris

Norwegian-born, London-based freelance photographer Cecilie Harris has had her work featured in magazines including *i-D*, photographing Olly Murs and The Feeling, and has photographed ad campaigns for the likes of Dinny Hall and Evisu. She is the editor-in-chief of *Boys by Girls*.

Cecilie found her calling at a young age, when she was still living in her hometown of Stavanger, Norway. When she was 12, her uncle, a photographer himself, gave her some photographs as a Christmas present. A few years later, she received her first SLR camera and would take pictures of the wooden houses in Stavanger, flowers and her friends. Selfies weren't yet in her vocabulary. The clean lines of the ocean's horizon and the Norwegian landscapes have stayed with her, and today her work has a recognizable simplicity.

'Life was simpler back then,' she says. 'Not only because I was a child with no worries, but because in the 1970s and '80s we weren't constantly exposed to a steady stream of news and information via mobile phones and the Internet. Now, of course, I don't know how I would live without these things. Growing up with slightly hippie parents meant that I felt like a strong and powerful woman very early on: I was carefree and unafraid of the world and my surroundings. If we wanted to swim naked in the sea, we would. With less access to media, we didn't have unrealistic ideals of the female body image. I was lucky to be able to focus my energy on doing my homework, practising the piano, going to ballet lessons and having a nice time with my friends. How wonderful it would be to have some of that simplicity back.'

Cecilie, how different is your childhood in Norway from your life today?

My life in London is miles apart from my life in Norway. As a 10-year-old, my days were spent exploring the seaside until I could hear my mum calling us home for bedtime – turning over rocks to look for crabs, lighting fires on the beach, building sand castles and competing with my friends to see who could eat the most ice cream. Remembering these moments feels like watching a film I haven't seen in a while, but that I would love to watch again. As a young girl I had the freedom to explore what was around me. I grew up at a time when kids could climb trees without a safety net or grown-ups around to catch you if you fell, and we were allowed to play on our own and build our own social networks. As a result, my imagination was always encouraged and I was very self-sufficient. Norway provided such a beautiful setting for an idyllic childhood: a little community of newly built housing by the fjord, a 15-minute drive to a sandy beach and a cottage by the ocean.

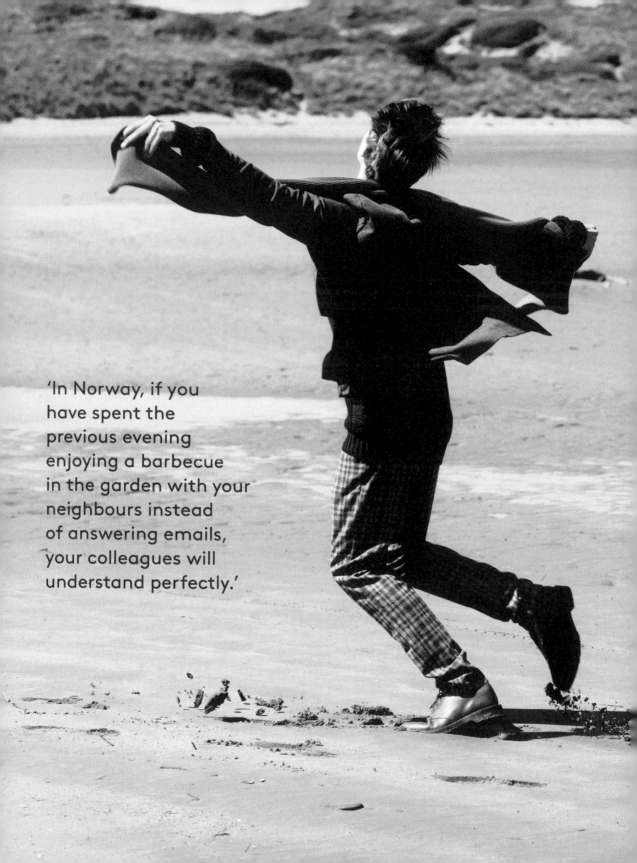

'In Norway, if you have spent the previous evening enjoying a barbecue in the garden with your neighbours instead of answering emails, your colleagues will understand perfectly.'

Is your photography inspired by your childhood memories of Norway?

Norway is very family orientated. The normal time to stop work is 4pm, which leaves more hours in the day for family and friends, and to simply enjoy time together. And the countryside is only a quick drive away, a place where you can de-stress, take in some fresh air and simply breathe. Even if you live in the city, you don't have to go very far to find these pockets of natural beauty. Living in London provides you with great parks and some of the richest cultural offerings there are, but getting out into the countryside takes forever and a trip to the seaside is such an effort. A four-hour tailback on the motorway to experience what I could simply walk to in Norway is often too much to handle.

As soon as spring comes and the sun is out, it is in any Norwegian's DNA to rush outside and enjoy it as much as possible. After months of being inside, sunny days are seen as a communal enjoyment. If you have spent the previous evening having a barbecue in the garden with your neighbours instead of answering emails, your colleagues will understand perfectly. There is a sort of unwritten, national understanding of time set aside for *hygge*.

As a Scandinavian living in London, how do you apply hygge *to your daily life?*

I try to as much as I can! I turn up the temperature inside my flat when it is cold outside, light some candles and snuggle under a blanket with a hot chocolate. I also surround myself as much as possible with people I can be honest with. Scandinavians like to talk openly about our lives once we have built up a trust with someone,

something that I have found more difficult to do in England. Talking about life and its ups and downs with a friend over a glass of wine, as you sit under a blanket on the rooftop, is crucial *hygge* time. I would simply go crazy if I go too long without those moments. If no one else is around, I am not afraid to enjoy some *hygge* time on my own.

Although it is easy to get wrapped up in busy city life, I try to be more aware of taking these moments now. It helps me to refocus my energy onto what I am doing. *Hygge* time can be spent by the seaside or inside a pub, accompanied by homemade cinnamon buns or a cheap bottle of wine and some cheese – it doesn't matter, as long as you're having quality time with a friend. I always have a few blankets ready for picnics or cold outdoor moments should the need arise. You can't take *hygge* out of a Scandinavian: it is ingrained in us.

Is there anywhere in Scandinavia that is particularly important to you?

My hometown of Stavanger! I grew up there, so my love for it is something that will always stay with me. It is on the southwest coast of Norway, so you get the ocean, easy access to the mountains and all the beautiful, unspoiled countryside you could wish for. Driving along the coast to Oslo, you pass all the cute towns in southern Norway, with white wooden houses as far as the eye can see. And if you drive from Stavanger to the north, you pass all the fjords and mountains. Having lived away from Norway for about 18 years, I am desperate to travel there more and visit some of the places I haven't seen for a while or have yet to visit. One day, when I am no longer a starving artist.

Edvard Munch

Forever identified with his most famous work, *The Scream*, Norwegian painter Edvard Munch (1863–1944) has had a profound influence on succeeding generations of artists. His work deals with issues of isolation and unease, and a peculiarly Scandinavian melancholy.

These days, everyone is familiar with the Nordic concept of feel-good cosiness, which represents for many the essence of Scandinavia's enduring appeal. An essential partner to *hygge* is its lesser known counterpart, *uhygge*, a sense of uneasiness or melancholy that descends when the nights draw in and the wind howls. In Scandinavian parlance, the 'blue hour' has arrived.

Perhaps the best represensor of *uhygge* – apart from the crime dramas that appear regularly on our televisions and in bookstores – is Edvard Munch, whose paintings, including *The Scream, The Sick Child* and *Melancholy*, tread the fine line between melancholia and horror. The early deaths from tuberculosis of his mother and elder sister, as well as the mental illness of another sister, and the oppressive religious atmosphere fostered by his father, probably contributed to Munch's unsettled, troubling view of the world. Munch himself was often ill as a child, and had bouts of madness and hallucinations, not helped by either grief or his father's disapproval of his interest in art. He abandoned his engineering studies and in 1881 enrolled at the Royal School of Art and Design in Oslo. Munch's early work did not meet with much success, and he was dependent on his father for financial support. His mental health suffered, and he began to drink heavily.

But Munch's fortunes were about to change. Although his naturalistic style, heavily influenced by the Post-Impressionists, did not find many admirers initially, salvation arrived in the form of a two-year state-funded scholarship to study in Paris. Munch arrived in France in 1889, at the time of the Exposition Universelle (his own *Morning*

was exhibited in the Norwegian pavilion), and studied under Léon Bonnat, professor at the École des Beaux-Arts. Success was not instant, but he began to work and exhibit steadily. In 1908 he experienced a severe mental breakdown, but recovered and spent the last two decades of his life in Norway. He died there just before the end of the Second World War, and remains an enigmatic figure who produced works of startling genius.

Helena Christensen

Danish model and photographer Helena Christensen is known the world over as one of the original supermodels of the 1990s. Today, her work is on the other side of the lens, and she has photographed for magazines including *Vogue* and *Harper's Bazaar*, as well as collaborating on projects with the United Nations High Commissioner For Refugees.

Helena Christensen's achievements need no introduction. Hers is one of the most recognizable faces in the world, and she is known to millions from countless magazine covers and appearances on the catwalk. In recent years, however, she has turned her attention to what goes on behind the camera, rather than in front of it.

Several exhibitions of her photography have been held, including *A Quiet Story* (2006–7) and *Far From, Close* (2008–9), the proceeds of which went to the International Centre of Photography and Chernobyl Children's Project International. She has recently been working on a series of portraits of women called *One with Nature*, and, as part of her charity work, is travelling with the United Nations High Commissioner For Refugees.

Helena, as a native of Denmark, is it important to recreate a Nordic atmosphere in your photographs?

The dark winter days and light summer nights of Scandinavia have always been a huge influence on my creativity. When the days are short and gloomy, and the wind howls, you just want to nest: it's all about blankets, fireplaces, cocoa and lots of candles. Somehow the darkness outside stimulates my brain. As a child, I would spend those times drawing, writing and reading. In the summer, the late-evening orange glow would keep me awake and I would go swimming or biking. Growing up in a country like Denmark, with its poetic landscape and tradition of cosiness, is a big part of why I became a photographer in the first place.

Now that you live abroad, what do you miss most about Denmark?

My family and the food, of course, but most of all the cosiness that you find everywhere in little, subtle ways, which is what is so special about Scandinavia. I tell people visiting Copenhagen to go to all our wonderful restaurants, and to visit the Tivoli Gardens, the neighbourhood of Christiania, Thorvaldsen Museum, the Louisiana Museum of Modern Art (p. 190), the waterfront district Nyhavn and the public square Kongens Nytorv. One of the best things about being a Dane is that we love to travel and experience the world. But we always keep Denmark in our hearts, and return back home for a taste of that *hygge*.

What elements of Scandinavian design most make you feel at home?

I am very proud of and fascinated by Scandinavian design. Our old-school furniture makers are geniuses: the way they created objects from a functional perspective, while at the same time infusing beauty, elegance and poetry, always draws me to their designs. The houses and cottages built in the 1950s and in the centuries before that are wonderful examples of great craftsmanship. I feel most at home when I'm at my summer beach cottage in the north, swimming in the ocean, late in the evening, as the sky changes into a dark orange and pink fire.

Karen Blixen

The novels, stories and letters of Danish author Karen Blixen (1885–1962), known to millions by her pseudonym Isak Dinesen, have been firm favourites in Scandinavia since the publication of *Seven Gothic Tales*, a collection of short stories, in 1934. Despite producing works such as *Out of Africa* and *Babette's Feast*, and being shortlisted, she never received the Nobel Prize for Literature. She died in 1962 in Denmark.

Karen Blixen was born into an affluent family, who lived at Rungstedlund, a country house in the small coastal town of Rungsted on the Øresund coast, just north of Copenhagen (it now houses the Karen Blixen Museum). Her father, Wilhelm Dinesen, a writer and army officer, had fathered a daughter, conceived while living among the Chippewa people in Wisconsin, and later had a child with the family's maid. Suffering from syphilis and depression, he hanged himself in the family home when Karen was nine.

In 1914 Karen Blixen married her second cousin, Baron Bror von Blixen-Finecke, and moved to Kenya, where they established a coffee plantation. The marriage was not happy, and Blixen contracted syphilis as a result of her husband's infidelities. By 1921, the couple had separated and Blixen took over running the farm. She and Bror were divorced in 1925, and Blixen embarked on a long-term love affair with Denys Finch Hatton, an English army officer and big-game hunter. After his death in an aeroplane accident in 1931, and the collapse of her business, Blixen, by this time financially ruined, returned to Rungstedlund, where she would write most of her novels and stories.

Blixen had already begun writing, but once in Denmark her new career began in earnest. A collection of short stories, *Seven Gothic Tales*, was published in 1934 under the name Isak Dinesen. It became a bestseller, and was followed by *Out of Africa* in 1937. Blixen's work was widely respected (Ernest Hemingway and Arthur Miller were admirers), and she was feted during her only visit to the United States in 1959, lunching with Marilyn Monroe and being photographed by Richard Avedon. Karen Blixen died in 1962 at the age of 77, but continues to be regarded among the great Scandinavian authors, and a champion of the Nordic way life, lived without fear or prejudice.

Les Gens Heureux

Only those in the know are able to find this contemporary art gallery, launched by Anneli Hakkinen and Sanne Frank in 2012 and located in the heart of Copenhagen. When visitors step off the lift at the fifth floor and into this former artist's atelier, they are immediately enveloped by that famous Nordic light – all the better for viewing the artworks on display.

Les Gens Heureux is located on Store Strandstræde, just a minute or two from the harbour, and housed at the top of a classically designed building from 1909, with high ceilings, huge windows and lots of space. Since its opening five years ago, the gallery has held art exhibitions and provided a meeting place for Copenhagen's creatives.

Anneli and Sanne founded the gallery both because of their love for art, and also because the location was perfect for the kind of space they wanted to create. 'You have to know it is there, so there is a secret, exclusive feeling about it,' says Anneli. 'The reaction people often have when they first visit is that they want to move in and live here. Since we are right under the roof, the gallery has a special feeling, full of *hygge*.'

Anneli, tell us about the unusual name of your gallery. Are you and Sanne influenced by Nordic art and artists in particular?

Sanne came up with the name (she came up with the name for Noma, too), which reflects the 'happy' feeling the gallery gives when you are inside it. It's also a bit ironic, with the implication that we are 'happy people' – which is what the Danes are known for, after all.

We are influenced by many Nordic artists, but if we had to name the one who influenced us the most in our choice of location, it would have to be Vilhelm Hammershøi (p. 212), as the gallery is filled with that amazing light that is such a feature of his work. We have been lucky in finding great artists, who have attracted equally great clients and press. Our favourite Nordic artists would, of course, be those we represent, including Mathias Malling Mortensen and Fie Norsker.

What exhibitions have you held recently at the gallery?

Recently, we had a solo exhibition of the work of the Serbian-born photographer, illustrator and product designer, Ana Kraš (see p. 186). Ana was in our first exhibition in 2012, and it was very special for us to finally have a solo show with her. Another recent exhibition featured the work of Peter Shire (left), a sculptor and furniture and ceramics designer. After that, perhaps more shows devoted to Nordic artists are on the cards!

What are some of the can't-miss highlights for a visitor to Copenhagen?

If you want to stay local, be sure to visit the Thorvaldsen Museum and the National Gallery of Denmark, as well as Ordrupgaard (p. 198). You should also head to the newly opened Copenhagen Contemporary on Papirøen (Paper Island), near the opera house. The Union Kitchen is a restaurant we go to often – it's cosy in the wintertime, but still hip, and is in the same building as our gallery. Otherwise Ved Stranden 10 for a glass of wine, and for its very *hyggeligt* interior. Or try Manfreds or Osteria 16, or head further afield to Sletten Havn in Humlebæk, or Hærværk in Aarhus – you won't be disappointed.

Louisiana Museum of Modern Art

This much-loved museum was founded by businessman Knud W. Jensen (who later became its first director), who originally intended it as a home for contemporary Danish art, but decided instead that it should have a more international scope, and feature works by artists from around the world. The museum opened its doors to the public in 1958.

The name of the museum does not refer to the American state of Louisiana, but to the three wives, all named Louise, of the buildings first owner, Alexander Brun, who built it in 1855. When Knud W. Jensen became the museum's director a century later, in 1958, there hadn't been a dedicated museum for Danes to see modern art, and he envisioned the Louisiana as a 'musical meeting place', a destination that engaged with contemporary life.

Jensen was famous for dividing exhibitions into 'hot' and 'cold': artworks that visitors were already familiar with were 'hot', while the work of new or emerging artists was 'cold'. This concept, now known as the 'sauna principle', attracts visitors with the reassuringly familiar, while also pushing them into seeing something new. The museum followed the model of the Museum of Modern Art in New York, which expanded its collection to include examples of architecture, design, film and photography, and sought to broaden visitors' horizons through unexpected groupings of works from different genres.

The Louisiana's great strength has always been its close relationship with the international arts scene, and is the primary reason why it has been possible to attract such a strong collection of celebrated artists. Many of the creatives featured in this book mention the Louisiana as one of their favourite places to visit, not just for the art on display, but also for the peaceful surroundings, leading down to the sea.

Moderna Museet

Located on the island of Skeppsholmen in the centre of Stockholm (with another branch in Malmø), this museum houses one of Europe's foremost collections of art from the 20th century to the present, including works by Picasso, Matisse, and a number of Nordic artists.

Since opening its doors in 1958, Moderna Museet has been known for its close relationships with artists and for attracting famous names to Stockholm. Its permanent collection includes works of Cubism, Dada and Surrealism, by artists such as Georges Braque, Juan Gris and René Magritte, as well as around 30 works by Marcel Duchamp, making the museum one of the largest repositories of his work in the world. Andy Warhol had his first solo exhibition in Europe here in 1968, and donations from art collectors, including Gerard Bonnier, have brought works by Yves Klein and Joan Miró.

One of the most important acquisitions has been a large group of works by Swedish and other Nordic artists, comprising over 4,000 individual items. The museum now has one of the largest collections in the world of Swedish art, including works by Öyvind Fahlström, Vera Nilsson, Siri Derkert, Dick Bengtsson, and many others.

Funding has traditionally been a challenge, but the implementation of such cultural policies as the Konstnärhjälpen, an artists' fund, money from the national lottery and other donations have swelled the coffers, enabling the museum to purchase more works by Scandinavian artists, including, importantly, work by Swedish female artists. Another important part of the development of the collection was the addition of 'The Museum of Our Wishes'.

The museum also has a busy restaurant, with stunning views towards Djurgården and Strandvägen, as well as a designated children's workshop, an important feature of Nordic museums, where children can experience art. Moderna Museet is not a hallowed place for solitude and quiet reflection, therefore, but a democratic meeting place, where children and adults alike gather together. A very Swedish philosophy, indeed.

Ordrupgaard

This museum, located in Charlottenlund, north of Copenhagen, came about when businessman and art collector Wilhelm Hansen (1868–1936) opened his magnificent collection to the public. Today the museum is under the guidance of director Anne-Birgitte Fonsmark, and continues Hansen's vision of bringing people together through art.

In 1916–18, Wilhelm Hansen and his wife Henny Soelberg Jensen, a former student, invited the public into their home on Sundays to view their magnificent art collection. A few years later, after the collapse of the Landmansbanken, Hansen had to sell half of his collection of French art, including works by Cézanne, Manet and Gauguin, many of which found their way into the Ny Carlsberg Glyptotek in Copenhagen.

Once his finances recovered, however, Hansen set about acquiring more works, including Delacroix's portrait of George Sand. Wilhelm Hansen died in 1936, and his widow continued to live in the house until her own death in 1951. She left the collection, the house and the park to the Danish government,

and in 1953 Ordrupgaard opened as a state-owned art museum. In 2005 a new extension, designed by the late Zaha Hadid, was added, and three years later the museum acquired the house of designer Finn Juhl (p. 34), located next door, which had been left to Ordrupgaard by Juhl's widow.

Anne-Birgitte, was William Hansen interested in Danish art, as well as French?

Wilhelm Hansen was among the first collectors of works by the Funen Painters, L. A. Ring and Vilhelm Hammershøi (p. 212). This interest in Danish Modernism, however, soon led to a passionate commitment to French art. More than anything else, Hansen is known for assembling a distinguished

collection of 19th-century French art, with works by Corot, Delacroix, Courbet, Manet, Monet, Pissarro, Renoir, Degas, Cézanne, Gauguin and Matisse. The collection was the antithesis of the Danish art scene at the time; Carl Jacobsen, the founder of Glyptotek, for example, focused on French academic art, to the exclusion of Impressionism.

How do you create harmony between the three very different buildings that form Ordrupgaard?

In 2005, when we added Zaha Hadid's extension, we were very conscious about creating a new building that had its own identity, but at the same time respected architect Gotfred Tvede's classicist design of the original house, which dates from the early 20th century. After the addition of Finn Juhl's House in 2008, which was built in 1942, the museum is both a monument to one of the biggest names in Danish design history and a physical expression of the development of Danish interior in the interwar years. A planned underground wing by the Norwegian architectural firm Snøhetta (p. 64), to be completed in 2019, will house Wilhelm and Henny Hansen's collection of French art.

How do you incorporate hygge *into the visitor experience at Ordrupgaard?*

Here, *hygge* is expressed through an unpretentious, homely environment. From the earliest building to the most recent, each is a manifestation of the Nordic approach of using simple materials, with no pomp and ceremony, and each created in harmony with the surrounding landscape. Ordrupgaard was known as a place where high society

came, including the Royal Family, but the estate was initially rural, unpretentious and relaxed. Zaha Hadid referenced the natural surroundings in her building, which hovers above ground, while Finn Juhl used simple, affordable materials in the design of his house. Eventually, Snøhetta's building will also welcome guests in a *hyggelig* atmosphere.

What events do you have planned at Ordrupgaard? And are there any secrets that visitors might not be aware of?

We have a number of upcoming special exhibitions planned, including shows devoted to the work of Claude Monet, L.A. Ring and his wife Sigrid Kähler, and an exhibition on Camille Pissarro and the Danish painter Fritz Melbye, which will explore links between painting of the Danish Golden Age and French Impressionism.

As for the museum's permanent collection, the French collection will transfer to Snøhetta's new building, allowing more room for the Danish art of Hammershøi and his time. While construction is going on, the French collection will travel abroad. In the park outside, Art Park Ordrupgaard features site-specific works by leading contemporary artists – including Carsten Höller, Klara Kristalova, Simon Starling and Jeppe Hein. We are currently expanding the Art Playground with a piece by Olafur Eliasson, alongside works by Doug and Mike Starn and Terunobu Fujimori.

Rose Eken

Having studied at the Edinburgh College of Art and the Royal College of Art in London, Danish artist Rose Eken is now a firmly established name on the Danish contemporary art scene. Her work, including *Frokosten (The Lunch)*, seen left, has been displayed in Scandinavia's leading galleries and museums.

As a child, Rose Eken was surrounded by artists. Her mother taught opera singers from their home, and her stepfather was a printmaker and owner of the art publisher Brøndums Forlag in Copenhagen. Rose left school at 16, and began working as a stage technician in a theatre and hanging out with punk and rock musicians – a period, she says, which has had a lasting influence on her work, instilling a fascination with the notion of space: venues, theatres, and the stories they tell when empty. She spent five years as a teenager taking drawing and art courses, and in 1997 applied to Edinburgh College of Art, where she spent the next four years. Afterwards, she graduated with a Master's in Visual Communications from the Royal College of Art in London.

Rose, do you think it is easier for you to work as an artist in Scandinavia, rather than in other countries?

In many ways, yes! In other ways, no – it's not easy to be an artist anywhere, but Denmark has a very good funding system through the Danish Arts Council, which supports emerging artists or artists with large-scale projects. Denmark also offers a three-year grant to a small group of artists each year, which is fundamental to building a strong and thriving art scene. I think it is one of the things we are good at as a nation, and something that is not really widely appreciated. Art has a profound effect on our society and on people's happiness.

Where do you find inspiration for new work?

I always find that a very hard question to answer. Inspiration comes from lots of different places and not always when you are looking for it! People, art and music are, of course, things that I'm around every day, but very banal things can inspire me, too: something I notice in the street, a dinner party, a conversation. Music is fundamental in shaping us, it moulds us in our formative years and helps us understand who we are as people. Music unites and divides us. We have all had an argument over some band or other, or have jumped up and down in front of a stage, screaming, along with 30,000 other people. In my work, I draw on this idea of collective memories from our shared modern music history and popular culture to evoke visually the ambience and mood that resonates within each of us.

Frokosten shows a typical Danish meal. Does it also represent your idea of Danish hygge?

For me, this work is perhaps more about taking something specific that we all relate to. The idea of a family gathering round a table is universal, and I aim to create scenes that resonate directly with the viewer. But, yes, the piece also represents something very Danish – open-faced sandwiches (*smørrebrød*), snaps and Royal Copenhagen porcelain are all at the core of our culture. So this work is definitely also a representation of Danish *hygge*.

Sigrid Bjorbekkmo

At only 27 years old, this photographer from the Norwegian archipelago of Vesterålen divides her time between photoshoots for magazines, studying for a degree in landscape architecture, and working on an exhibition in Los Angeles. She is based in Oslo.

Sigrid comes from a small town in the islands of Vesterålen, in northern Norway, which are known for their beautiful and dramatic landscapes. When she was 16, she went to Italy for a year and came back with new language skills and an interest in photography. She began documenting her friends, and spent hours browsing through other people's photographs on Flickr. In 2011 she enrolled in the Bilder Nordic School of Photography in Oslo.

'Most of my photographs are influenced by the light and desaturated colours of Norway,' she says. 'I almost always shoot in natural light, very rarely in direct sunlight. The light changes a lot throughout the year. One series, *Shorter Days*, was inspired by the gloomy November days and lack of sunlight. Some of my images also convey a mood and feeling of nostalgia. I am calm and quite quiet, which is reflected in the way I shoot and edit my images.'

Sigrid, do you think that your home country has influenced your photography?

Although I spent most of my teenage years wishing I lived somewhere, anywhere, else, I keep thinking back to the place I grew up in for inspiration. Having a bit of time and distance has opened my eyes to tfhe beauty of the landscape that I used to take for granted. Other than that, I love to photograph wherever I travel, in Norway or beyond. Sometimes I need to get out of my comfort zone and see new things. It doesn't have to be too far, though – discovering new streets and neighbourhoods in Oslo can be very inspiring.

'Autumn, for me, is about curling up under a blanket indoors, drinking coffee or wine with friends or watching a favourite show on television, putting on lots of layers and going for walks in the countryside.'

Do you have any favourite ways of applying hygge *to your everyday life?*

For me, *hygge* has a lot to do with the colder months, and autumn in particular, when we put on lots of layers and go for long walks in the outdoors. One of the great things about Oslo is that it is so close to the woods, the beach and the islands. There are also plenty of great bars and cafés, so when it gets colder, that's where I head to. Many of my favourites are in neighbourhoods away from the shopping streets and touristy areas.

In the summer, we ride our bikes to the beach, swim off the piers, or hang out in one of Oslo's many parks, drinking beer.

What projects are you working on at the moment?

Right now I am working on editorial assignments for national and international magazines, many of which involve portraits, which I really enjoy shooting. I will also be participating in a collective exhibition in Los Angeles with other female photographers and artists.

Although I love photography, I actually almost love it more when I have other things to focus on, as well. When I am not working, I study landscape architecture. I think the two subjects are closely related and equally interesting, and I hope to combine them in the future. Perhaps in 10 years I will have opened a landscape architecture/ photography studio with some classmates! Who knows?

Vilhelm Hammershøi

This Danish artist is revered for his subtle use of colour in portraying the Scandinavian interior – particularly his own home at Strandgade 30 in Copenhagen. While living there, Vilhelm Hammershøi (1864–1916) created a body of work that would have a profound influence on Danish art, design and architecture in the 20th century.

In Vilhelm Hammershøi's poetic and understated paintings of interiors, light and time seem to stand still. The interior he painted most often, Strandgade 30 in Copenhagen, is where he lived from 1898 to 1909 with his wife, Ida Ilsted, who often appears as a quiet, ghostly figure in his work (including this painting, opposite, from 1901). Hammershøi's paintings might not exemplify *hygge*, with their cold, empty blue light, echoing the Nordic winter, but rather a balance between *hygge* and *uhygge*.

Hammershøi studied with P.S. Krøyer (see p. 234) from 1883 to 1885, when he showed *Portrait of a Young Girl* at the Charlottenborg Spring Exhibition, where it reputedly caught the eye of Renoir. He painted at home, rather than in a studio, and often the same interiors, with Ida as his model, rearranging the furniture to create variation. But although Hammershøi painted his home, his paintings, in contrast to the prevailing trend of the time, were not wholly concerned with domesticity. The subtle tones of grey and blue create enigmatic spaces, filled with melancholy and loneliness, reinforced by the stillness of the interiors.

In 2001, the Metropolitan Museum of Art in New York held an exhibition devoted to the work of Vilhelm Hammershøi, and retrospectives of his work have also been held at the Musée d'Orsay in Paris and the Guggenheim Museum in New York. In 2008, the Royal Academy in London held the first major exhibition in Britain of his work. Hammershøi's only painting on permanent display in the UK is *Interior* in the National Gallery, painted in 1898.

Travel
&
Nature

Allmannajuvet

The zinc mines at Allmannajuvet, sited along a National Tourist Route between Sauda and Hellandsbygda in Norway, date back to 1881. They fell into disuse in 1899, with the advancements in hydropower technology and the establishment of manufacturing elsewhere. In 2002, Swiss architect and Pritzker Prize-winner Peter Zumthor was asked to redesign the site as a visitors' centre, incorporating a museum, café and parking facilities.

The mines had once played an important role in the economic fortunes of this part of southern Norway, and a major employer in the region, but had lain derelict since closing a mere 17 years after they opened. When the Norwegian Public Roads Administration decided to renovate the site, Peter Zumthor was asked to design buildings that were in tune with the surrounding landscape.

The complex is formed of three modest buildings: a museum dedicated to the history of mining, a café, and a service building near the main road. An adjoining car park was also added, with a curving stone wall that follows the Storelva river. The cold, somewhat isolated feeling of the site is suggestive of a certain loneliness and melancholy: *uhygge*, the opposite of *hygge*, the feeling you get when something unfamiliar or scary might be lurking around the corner, or when far away from family and friends.

But the redevelopment has brought warmth and togetherness back to the site, offering a unique and memorable day out for visitors and families that incorporates the warm cosiness of a wooden hut and vast tracts of snowy, forested landscape. Now part of the Ryfylke Museum, the complex opened in 2016.

Christoffers Blommor

Having begun as a one-man venture in 2001, Christoffers Blommor is now one of Stockholm's most popular florists. Owner Christoffer Broman's passion is wildflowers, long before they became trendy, and creates bouquets inspired by the fields and meadows of Scandinavia.

'When I started the shop in 2001, I never dreamed that I would be running it for so long,' Christoffer says. 'It was a struggle at first – I didn't have any experience of buying flowers at market or of boring paperwork – but I felt immediately that this shop was special. Our customers are like friends: in the early days they would stop by for a chat and buy flowers to support me. After a couple of years of seven-day weeks and long hours, my friend Sarah came on board, which allowed me to be able to get to market early and buy the best flowers.'

Once Christoffers Blommor was firmly established, those early customers were joined by new clients, all of whom form a vital part of the local community network. 'We still work with our old clients, including Rigmor, a 92-year-old lady who loves roses and has been a customer from the start,' says Christoffer. 'We also work with fashion brand Acne Studios and with magazine stylists and bloggers, and need to please them all. That's why we buy fresh flowers every day. We don't keep them in a cooler: we have them placed all over the store, which is only 19 m² (205 sq ft). Sarah is still by my side after 10 years, and we have a wonderful staff of seven who work in both stores, at Gamla Stan and Södermalm, a very trendy area next to the Grandpa store and Il Caffe, from whom we rent our space. There are no doors between us, so you can grab a coffee on your way out.'

Christoffer, do you think that flowers are an essential part of hygge in Swedish homes?
Swedes are wonderful at making their homes cosy. We often buy flowers at the weekend (especially on Fridays, a bouquet called *fredagsbuketten*), when we invite family and friends round for meals. So flowers,

dinner, candles and friends: that sums up *hygge* in Stockholm. As far as trends go, we love the wild look of natural bouquets: no stiff flowers, like gerberas, or artificial ones. We also use a lot of peonies, baby's breath and astrantia, although I think our favourites are Persian fritillaries, French tulips and ranunculus. We pick the best the seasons have to offer and then do our magic.

Are some seasons more popular than others for flowers?

Flowers are popular all year around. Sweden is filled with wildflowers from May to August, and spring is especially wonderful, with tulips, ranunculus and anemones. Midsummer's Eve is also great for us, with all the flower crowns and table arrangements. In the summer, like the rest of Sweden, we shut up shop for the holidays.

Which of your favourite flowers can be found locally?

Tulips are grown outside Stockholm, so it's close to the shop. The quality is very good, with a huge variety in types and colours. We also have a lot of nice flowers in pots, like hydrangeas, bulbs in the spring and pelargonium.

What flowers should we use for making a Midsummer wreath?

A good *midsommarkrans* is a wild one! Start by making a shape with a wire or thread, then add plenty of grass-like herbs and any flowers you like. This year we used a lot of rosemary, mint and chamomile, and then mixed in some beautiful veronicas and cornflowers. There are no rules: just think about making it last until the early hours. It's a big party night in Sweden!

Ekebergparken

This sculpture and national heritage park, set up by the Norwegian art collector Christian Ringnes in 2013, boasts one of the most extensive and impressive collections of public art in the world – and has been named by the *Wall Street Journal* as one of its top-five sculpture parks. Among the works on display are sculptures by Salvador Dalí, Fernando Botero, Marina Abramović and Damien Hirst.

rebels, the Birkebeiners, and landed near Eikabergstøa, below Ekebergskråningen. Three hundred years later, another battle was fought at Ekeberg, between Swedish and Norwegian forces on Svenskesletten in 1567, during the Northern Seven Years' War (although initially successful, the Swedes were eventually defeated). And along the mountain ridges from the south and over Ekeberget runs the oldest road to Oslo, over which people have travelled for more than 10,000 years.

In more recent times, Ekebergskråningen was made into a park in 1889. With a heavy concentration of factories in the eastern side of Oslo, it became clear that a local park was needed to provide factory workers with access to fresh air and leisure time. Nearly 60 years later, during the Second World War, the Germans laid more than 5,000 mines on Ekebergsletta, and it is still possible to see markings on the tree trunks in the nearby woods, indicating their position.

Today, the sculpture park welcomes millions of visitors all year round, and showcases both international artists, including Rodin and Renoir, alongside such notable Norwegian sculptors as Knut Steen, Per Ung and Per Inge Bjørlo.

The Ekeberg neighbourhood of Oslo has a long history that reaches back to the days when Scandinavia developed from a hunter-gatherer to a farming society. The remains of stone walls, made when the land was originally cleared of rocks, are still visible in the ground, marking the border between cultivated and uncultivated land.

In the centuries that followed, a single monarch supplanted the local kings and chieftains, and the old Norse religion began to die away. In 1240, an uprising led by a nobleman, Skule Bårdsson, resulted in the Battle of Oslo – a battle that would have a profound effect on Norwegian history. King Haakon IV arrived by sea with a party of

'Ekebergparken stands as a democratic gift to society, giving both locals and visitors access to great art and the great outdoors.'

Ett Hem

This private residence-turned-hotel, built in 1910, is located in a quiet residential area of Stockholm. Named by the *Telegraph* newspaper as one of the 50 greatest hotels in the world, Ett Hem is not your typical hotel destination. Staying here is a cosy experience, and testament to the skills of its half-Danish, half-Canadian interior designer, Ilse Crawford.

For owner Jeanette Mic, it was important that Ett Hem both retained its historic personality and catered to the requirements of modern-day travellers. The hotel has furniture by some of the most influential Scandinavian makers, including Hans J. Wegner, as well as Ilse Crawford's own designs, and each of the 12 guestrooms are different, with one containing an enormous, handpainted stove and wood panelling.

'It's on a smaller scale than other hotels, so automatically it feels more friendly,' says Ilse. 'We wanted to create somewhere that amplifies the life you have when staying here. When we start a project, we always address the location. We want to bring it to life by looking at its history, or where it is right now.'

In keeping with the ethos of Nordic living, the food on offer is fresh, local and seasonal, with the menu changing daily, and served round the clock. Guests can have their meals in the greenhouse overlooking the garden or in the more formal setting of the library, and are encouraged to pop into the kitchen for a snack.

In the spirit of Scandinavian transport, guests can also borrow bicycles and explore Stockholm and its many museums and attractions. Under Jeanette and Ilse's expert guidance, Ett Hem provides the quintessential Nordic experience of cosy homeliness, and a comfortable base for anyone wishing to explore one of Scandinavia's great cities.

Gaularfjellet

Gaularfjellet is a mountainous region in Norway, located off the spectacular 80 km (50 mile)-long Fylkesvei 13. Perched high on the peaks, overlooking the Vetlefjord below, is the Viewpoint, a triangular concrete viewing platform jutting out into the landscape by Norwegian architectural firm Code. With panoramic views and poised 700 m (2,300 ft) above sea level, a climb to the top is not for the fainthearted.

Plans to build a road over the Gaularfjellets had been mooted since 1853, but it would be another hundred years before they would be realized. Today, the road provides a tranquil place for experiencing the vast landscape, in sharp contrast to its previous role in the 1930s as an important transport route.

Previously a well-kept secret, Gaularfjellet offers those in the know a stunning journey across the mountains between Dragsvik and the Sognefjord. One of the few protected waterways in Norway is Gaularvassdraget, with waterfalls and wild rapids. Visitors can follow the 25 km (15.5 mile)-long path around the basin, from Nystølen to Eldal, for the full immersion into the wild beauty of the Scandinavian countryside.

Once they've clambered to the top of the viewing platform, intrepid climbers will experience a feeling of flying, or standing at the prow of a ship. 'The structure is a triangular concrete surface, with corners pointing towards north, south and west,' say the architects. 'Each corner is shaped specifically in relation to the landscape and to a different use. The goal was to create a shape that stimulates physical movement and works as an arena for cultural events. All of the necessary energy is provided by solar panels, placed on the west point.'

Helenekilde

Holidays by the seaside have been a popular Danish pastime for over a hundred years, and immortalized on canvas by the artists that congregated around the port town of Skagen, on the Jutland peninsula. Today, over 40 of these traditional hotels are in business today, and remain popular spots for seaside holidays.

The seaside hotels that flourished here in the early 20th century serve as a lasting reminder of those artists, including P. S. Krøyer, who captured the light and sunshine of Nordic summer afternoons by the sea.

Many of these old seaside hotels give the illusion of having been frozen in the early 1900s, when well-heeled guests would have stayed all summer. Helenekilde, located on the northern tip of Zealand and overlooking the Kattegat Sea, is no exception. While the artists are long gone, Denmark's *badehoteller* serve as a lasting reminder of those painters, particularly P. S. Krøyer (left and previous pages), who captured the light and sunshine of Nordic summer afternoons by the seaside.

Today, Helenekilde, with its relaxed, easygoing atmosphere, is one of the most popular. 'The focus is on good food in pleasant surroundings with sea views, a kind of quiet luxury,' says owner Alexander Kølpin, who bought the building in 2001. It was originally the private residence of construction tycoon Sir Grüner, who gave the house to his wife in 1896. As the area grew in popularity as a holiday destination, it was converted into a guesthouse in 1904, with another wing added in 1968.

At Helenekilde, guests can enjoy a drink on the terrace, soak up the view while reclining on sun loungers in the garden, or descend the stairs down to the beach, directly beneath the hotel, for a swim in the surf. As most of the Nordic countries are surrounded by miles of coastline, growing up in Scandinavia means plenty of family outings to the beach or travel to neighbouring countries by boat, and a stay here reinforces that all-important connection to water. An essential part of the Nordic way of living is that time set aside for recreation and space is as important as work, to free the mind and make room for imagination and pleasure.

Oslovelo

This café/bike shop in Oslo is the place cycling enthusiasts head to when they are not busy riding their bikes, and is also welcoming to non-cyclists. At Oslovelo, customers can pick up parts and accessories to customize their bikes, get advice on a project, repair a puncture, join a social event, buy a gift or enjoy a drink with friends.

Oslovelo was founded by a group of friends with a shared love of cycling and mutual backgrounds in restaurants and bike shops, as well as the desire to strike out on their own and go into business for themselves. With the aim of creating a quality café/bar with workshop attached, the friends opened their first space in 2014, in the semi-hidden backyard of a flat in the Oslo neighbourhood of Grünerløkka, working for free and putting all of the money they earned back into the company. Managing to save enough to move to larger premises, they began looking around for a suitable space, before finding this building in the conservation area of Birkelunden. Oslovelo opened its doors to grateful cyclists in 2016.

Why do you think cycling plays such a big part in Nordic culture?

We wouldn't put Norway at the forefront of the cycling movement, but we're getting there. Cities are getting a lot more crowded and difficult to move around in, so the bicycle is a natural choice. Not only is it the quickest way to get around, it's also the 'greenest' way, which is becoming more and more important. We're always working on something, whether a custom rebuild, producing the third generation of our bike line (the first was OK Bikes, the second OSL Bikes), teaching courses, baking and developing new bread and pizza recipes, holding bike races, book launches, poetry readings, exhibitions – you name it! We're always up for a good time.

If we dropped into the café today, what would we find?

Each day we offer two sandwich options, one of which is always vegetarian. We bake everything in-house, and try to get most of our ingredients locally. We get our coffee beans from Supreme Roastworks. They're just across the park, so we can cycle there and get our supplies. In the evening, we offer an expanded menu that includes flatbread pizzas and nachos with two types of melted cheese, along with our very own strawberry salsa. Being a neighbourhood joint, we also offer beer from Brygghus, which is just a stone's throw away, and we work closely with our friends at Vin John, who source their wines from small producers.

Where do you head to in Norway to get away from it all?

If you want to experience the great outdoors, Norway is full of it! Hiking in Jotunheimen and skiing or cycling at Finse are top of the list. As for Oslo, some of our favourite places to eat out are Brutus, Kampen Bistro, Hell's Kitchen or Smalhans; top of the list are Maaemo (p. 126), Way Down South, Taco República or Hitchhiker. For a drink, head to Parkteatret, Human Mote, Torggata Botaniske, Last Train, Bar Robinet, Rouleur or Internasjonalen. And as for seeing the sights, just get on your bike! There are plenty of scenic routes, too: hit Maridalen for long stretches of quiet roads; Aker Brygge for ferries to the islands around the city; or out to Nesodden, along the sea.

Sandqvist

This Swedish company, founded in 2004, caters to travellers who enjoy the outdoors and require a practical rucksack that is both durable and stylish. Citing the forests and rivers of the Nordic countryside as their primary inspiration, its three leaders – founder Anton Sandqvist, brother Daniel and their friend Sebastian – have produced collections for Hasselblad, Hensch and Volvo, among others, and now supply more than 500 retailers in over 30 countries.

Anton Sandqvist got the idea for setting up his own company after discovering that he couldn't find a good work bag. At first, the range of bags he offered wasn't very extensive, but after being joined by Daniel and Sebastian, he began to produce more varied and contemporary designs, inspired by the trio's shared interest in the outdoors.

'The Scandinavian countryside can be quite inhospitable, but also very beautiful, and we want our bags to reflect this,' Sebastian explains. 'We make quality bags with a timeless design that are functional and have a clear Nordic heritage. For us, Nordic design is about letting the materials and quality do the talking. A backpack is something you use to carry stuff in, but why use something that doesn't look and feel good?'

Sebastian, do you collaborate with other brands and designers?

We do! Two recent collaborations that we are particularly proud of are with Volvo and Hasselblad. For Volvo, we produced two collections: one of premium bags, made using vegetable-tanned leather and a bit more high end; the other is more outdoorsy/urban, made from Cordura with details in vegetable-tanned leather. The collection for Hasselblad consists of two functional and stylish camera bags in Cordura and one premium leather tote bag. We are very proud of both of these partnerships.

Where would you recommend going to experience the best of the Swedish outdoors?

Our favourite spot in Sweden is Härjedalen, about a seven-hour drive north of Stockholm. The area is very unpopulated, with mountains, rivers, lakes and forests. It's the perfect getaway if you want to go fishing, hiking, skiing, mountain biking, or just have some time off.

What projects are you working on or developing at the moment?

We have lots of fun things in the pipeline! We are currently trying out fabrics and shapes for the new collection, and are planning on opening our second flagship store outside of Sweden. The last one we opened was in 2016, in London. And there's some stuff in progress that I can't talk about just yet. Keep your eyes and ears open!

Scandinavian Airlines

For over 70 years, SAS (as it is often shortened to) has been the primary means of international travel for Scandinavians. In the wake of the Second World War, a new world of travel and of glamorous adventure beckoned, both abroad and to the newly accessible furthest reaches of the Nordic countries.

Founded in 1946, SAS became the first airline to schedule flights on the polar route, a journey that became popular with Hollywood celebrities and American tourists, and led to increased travel to the Nordic countries. The airline soon commissioned Christian Dior to design the uniforms, which echoed the designer's revolutionary 'New Look'. The company subsequently worked with other acclaimed designers, including French couture house Carven, and Calvin Klein, whose ultra-modern designs were in keeping with the Scandinavian take on minimalism and fashion.

In the 1950s and '60s, air travel was still a luxury, and eating on board was an experience in fine dining. From the start, the airline concentrated on combining Scandinavian ingredients with international trends, serving up dishes such as jellyfish marinated in Pernod and served with roasted prawns, and oysters in freeze-dried seawater, cotton candy and yuzu, all eaten with cutlery designed by Sigurd Persson. The company's eye for design also extended to its hotel, the SAS Hotel in Copenhagen, which still contains the original 1960s furniture designed by Arne Jacobsen.

A recent collaboration with Noma restaurant resulted in the book *Flavour: A Journey in Scandinavian Taste*, an exploration of New Nordic cuisine and its emphasis on quality ingredients, natural resources, cultural heritage and the desire to experiment. The airline's attention to detail in all areas – from the specially designed uniforms and cutlery to hotels – celebrates the Nordic tradition of well-designed surroundings and emphasis on stylish comfort.

'SAS was the first airline to schedule flights on the polar route, a journey that became popular with Hollywood celebrities and American tourists, and led to increased travel to the Nordic countries.'

Treehotel

Kent Lindvall, a former vocational guidance counsellor, and his wife Britta Jonsson-Lindvall were determined to live and work in the Lapland village where they grew up, in the northern reaches of Sweden. 'We love our village,' Britta explains, 'so we looked at what we could do with what we have here.' The result is Treehotel, an unusual hotel comprising seven 'rooms', with the most recent designed by Norwegian architectural firm Snøhetta (p. 64).

'One day, the filmmaker Jonas Selberg Augustsén, who has connections to the area, came to the guest house,' says Kent. 'Over the course of the summer, he and his team shot *Trädälskaren (The Tree Lover)*, about three city dwellers who want to go back to nature, and build a treehouse together.'

When filming was complete, Britta thought it would be a shame to let such a nice treehouse go to waste. At the time, Kent was on a fishing trip in Russia with a group of friends, who just happened to be three of Sweden's foremost architects: Bertil Harström, Thomas Sandell and Mårten Cyren. Kent mentioned the idea of a boutique hotel with specially designed rooms, which caught the interest of his friends, and by the end of the trip each of them had agreed to design a room apiece, even though they were working for competing firms. Their friendly collaboration turned out to be a key factor in the development of Treehotel.

Seven 'treehouses' were designed, including Dragonfly (above) and Mirror Cube (opposite), and immediately attracted local and international attention. Design aficionados from all over the world began coming to the Treehotel in large numbers to experience the unique design and layout.

'Treehotel has grown like a jigsaw puzzle, the result of resolute goals, hard work, timing, contacts, a sense for trends, an ability to capture the quirky and crazy in life, a penchant for personal service and Britta's motto that things will always work out in the end,' says Kent. 'They always do.'

Directory

Photo credits

t: top; m: middle; b: bottom; bk: back; f: front

2 Dieter Meyrl; 4 Sara Gelfgren; 6 Vilhelm Hammershøi, *Dust Motes Dancing in Sunbeams*, 1900 (Ordrupgaard Museum); photo Pernille Klemp; 7t Stutterheim; 7m Anders Schønnemann; 7b Royal Copenhagen/Fiskars; photo © Graae, Armgaard & Bangsbo Photography; 8–9 Tuuka Koshi; 10 File Under Pop; 12 Jeppe Sørensen Fotografi; 13 Erik Olsson; 14–15 Svenskt Tenn; 16 Susanne Bojesen Rosenqvist; 17bk Artilleriet; photo Fanny Hansson; 17f Sara Gelfgren; 18 Pernille Klemp; 19–23 www.designmuseum.dk Photo: Pernille Klemp; 24–9 Artilleriet; photos Fanny Hansson; 30–3 Rosendahl Group/Bjørn Wiinblad; photos Bjarni B. Jacobsen Fotografi; 34 Sara Gelfgren; 35–7 Henrik Sørensen; 38t Finn Juhl/Ordrupgaard, www.houseoffinnjuhl.com; 38b Susanne Bojesen Rosenqvist; 39 Henrik Sørensen; 40 Royal Copenhagen/Fiskars; 41 © Graae, Armgaard & Bangsbo Photography; 42–3 Royal Copenhagen/Fiskars; 44–7 Svenskt Tenn; 48–51 File Under Pop; 52–5 Mads Nørgaard; 56–7 Design Museum Denmark; photos Pernille Klemp; 58–9 designmuseum.dk Photo: Pernille Klemp; 60–1 Skandinavisk; 63bk Helenekilde Badehotel; 63f Skandinavisk; 64–7 © Ketil Jacobsen; 68–73 Alastair Philip Wiper; 74–78bk Stilleben; 78f Maja Flink; 79 Stilleben; 80 Whistles and Stutterheim; 81 © Bohman & Sjöstrand Ab; 82 © Niklas Lello; 83 Superunion; 85 Arne Langleite; 86 Sara Gelfgren; 88–9 Uh La La Ceramics; photos Peter Salinas; 90–1 Inger Marie Grini. All rights reserved. www.ingermariegrini.

no; 92–3 Grete Sivertsen; 95t Inger Marie Grini. All rights reserved. www.ingermariegrini.no; 95b Niklas Hart; 96 Freya McOmish; 97bk Anders Schønnemann; 97f Sara Gelfgren; 98 Sara Gelfgren; 99 Freya McOmish; 100l Mikkel Heriba; 100r Freya McOmish; 101 Mikkel Heriba; 102–5 Anders Schønnemann; 106–15 Erik Olsson erik@eof.se +46 708 31 06 08; 116–19 Claes Bech-Poulsen; 120 Lars Petter Pettersen; 121–4 Restaurant Kontrast; 125 Lars Petter Pettersen; 126–7 Tuuka Koshi; 128–9 Bandar Abdul Jauwad; 130–1 Tuuka Koshi; 132–3 Mielcke & Hurtigkarl; 134–5 Marie Louise Munkegaard; 136bk Ivar Kvall; 136f–41 Anders Schønnemann; 142 Rasmus Malmstrøm; 143 Camilla Stephan & Rasmus Malmstrøm; 144–5 Mikkeller Press; 146–7 Camilla Stephan; 148–51 Sofie Barfoed; 152–7 Per-Anders Jörgensen; 158 Sara Gelfgren; 159–60 Signe Roderik and Studio Restaurant; 161 Ole Haupt; 162 Velo Coffee; 163 Sara Gelfgren; 164 Vilhelm Hammershøi, *Interiør with Young Woman, Seen from Behind*, 1903–4 (Randers Kunstmuseum); photo Pernille Klemp; 165 File Under Pop; illustration by Sara Gelfgren; 166–7 Mads Nørgaard Archive; 168bl Mads Nørgaard Archive; 168–9 Andreas Emenius; 170–1 Sune Czajkowski; styling by Dorothea Gundtoft for the Red Cross; 172–7 Cecilie Harris; 178 Edvard Munch, *Nude sitting on a sofa*, 1925–6 (© Munchmuseet, Oslo); photo Sidsel de Jong; 179 Edvard Munch, *Man sitting on a bench (Rolf Hansen)*, 1943 (© Munchmuseet, Oslo); photo Svein Andersen; 180 Helena Christensen; 181 Caroline Brasch Nielsen; 183 Helena Christensen; 184–5 Karen Blixen Museum Rungstedlund; 186 Anders Sune Berg; 187 Amateurs, *A*

Flag for Every Home (03), 2014; 188t Peter Shire, *Still Life: Lemons, Oranges and Watermelon*, 1992; 188b Peter Shire, *Type Sorts with Cheese*, 2014; 189 Anna Topuriya, *Hot Air Rises II*, 2012; 190, 192, 193 Louisiana Museum of Modern Art; 191 Kim Hansen; 194 Fotograf Åke E:son Lindman AB Maria Bangata 4A 118 63 Stockholm +46 8 343580 info@lindmanphotography.com; 195–7 Moderna Museet and Åke Eson Lindman; 198 Adam Mørk; 199 Ordrupgaard; 201 © 2015. All rights reserved; 202–5 Rose Eken; 206–11 Fotograf Sigrid Bjorbekkmo; 213 Vilhelm Hammershøi, *Interior with Piano*, 1901 (Ordrupgaard Museum); photo Pernille Klemp; 214 Peter Lundström/WDO; 215 Skandinavisk; illustration by Sara Gelfgren; 216 Statens vegvesen; 217 © Foto: Per Berntsen; 218–21 Johan Lygrell; 222–5 Ivar Kvall; 226–31 Ett Hem; 232–3 National Tourist Routes, Jiri Havran, Jarle Wæhler, Samuel Hoang, wanderingaway.com; Code Architects; 234–5 P.S. Krøyer, *Summer's Day on Skagen's Southern Shore*, 1884 (Hirschsprung Collection); 236t P.S.Krøyer, *Summer Evening at Skagen Beach. The Artist and his Wife*, 1899 (Hirschsprung Collection); 236b P.S.Krøyer, *Self-portrait* (Hirschsprung Collection); 237 Tine Hvolby; 238 Sara Gelfgren; 239–41 Christian Olstad and Scott De Castro; 242–5 Sandqvist; 246 SAS; 247t ©Fritz Hansen 2002; 247m Sigurd Persson cutlery, SAS; www.sigurdpersson.se; 247b–9 SAS; 250–3 Peter Lundström/WDO

Dorothea Gundtoft is a contributor to *Vogue*, ELLE award-winner and author of *New Nordic Design* and *Fashion Scandinavia*, both published by Thames & Hudson. She is based in Copenhagen.

For my husband-to-be, Niels Arnth-Jensen

On the cover: *Front and back* Ceramics by Ragnhild Wik, WIK Oslo. Photo by Inger Marie Grini.

Designed by Sandra Kaas Greve
Drawings by Sara Gelfgren

First published in 2017 in the United States of America by Thames & Hudson Inc., 500 Fifth Avenue, New York, New York 10110

www.thamesandhudsonusa.com

Library of Congress Control Number 2017931854

ISBN 978-0-500-29279-2

Printed and bound in China by Toppan Leefung Printing Limited